FOUR LECTURES

THE
BAGLEY
WRIGHT
LECTURE
SERIES

LISA JARNOT

FOUR
LECTURES

WAVE BOOKS

SEATTLE AND NEW YORK

Published by Wave Books

www.wavepoetry.com

Wave Books titles are distributed to the trade by

Consortium Book Sales and Distribution

Phone: 800-283-3572 / SAN 631-760X

Library of Congress Cataloging-in-Publication Data

Names: Jarnot, Lisa, 1967– author.

Title: Four lectures / Lisa Jarnot.

Description: First edition. | Seattle : Wave Books, 2024. |

Series: Bagley Wright lecture series | Includes bibliographical references.

Identifiers: LCCN 2023041554 | ISBN 9781950268924 (paperback)

Subjects: LCSH: Jarnot, Lisa, 1967– | Poetry—Appreciation. |

Poetics. | LCGFT: Lectures. | Essays.

Classification: LCC PS3560.A538 F68 2024 | DDC 814/.54

[B]—dc23/eng/20230911

LC record available at https://lccn.loc.gov/2023041554

Designed by Crisis

Printed in the United States of America

9 8 7 6 5 4 3 2 1

First Edition

Out of paint make light, like a painter.

STEPHEN RODEFER, *Four Lectures*

FOUR LECTURES

I

WHITE MEN, WHITE WHALES,
AND WHITEHEAD

"Shepherds are honest people; let them sing!"
GEORGE HERBERT, "Jordan (I)"

ONE

I should begin by saying that my capacity for earnestness is either my super power or my fatal flaw. And given this very terrific opportunity to delve into my life and work as a poet, I'm just going to let it all hang out tonight, and I'm hoping that you find something useful in the earnestness and not something dreadful in it (as my eleven-year-old daughter so often does). This is the first of four lectures that I'll be presenting over a period of four seasons, and I've decided to frame this sequence of talks not only as a "call story" and testimony about my own work but also equally importantly as a testimony about a tradition in American poetry that has absolutely sustained me and, it would be appropriate to say, has absorbed me into it (as much as I have absorbed it) over the last thirty-five years.

When I think about what this tradition is, which we might call an American "experimental" or "open verse" poetry originating out of Whitman and Dickinson (and before that, on the other side of the ocean, out of William Blake), I know for me that it has always been populated with white men, white whales (as in Melville's in the novel *Moby-Dick*, 1851), and Whitehead (as in Alfred North Whitehead and particularly his cosmological treatise *Process and Reality*, 1929). This might seem like a seriously complicated barrel of monkeys, and I think it is, yes, but I'd like to frame it as something to explore and to be curious about tonight.

The other thing I want to be clear about from the beginning of this talk is that I am not a fancy poet even as I invoke these big books by Melville and Whitehead. I don't want to wield these texts as intellectual currency; I want to use them to tell a tale. I seem to have the mind of a poet, which makes me good at poaching and weaving, and not so inclined to traditionally academic discourse. This leads me to a second note, which is that I'm also a "townie," as poet Ron Silliman once called me, meaning that, like him, I'm a local yokel who found my way into an intellectual world by the accident of being in the right low-tuition public university at the right time: in his case, UC Berkeley in the 1960s, and, in my case, SUNY Buffalo in the 1980s.

TWO

It seems to me that the inspiration behind poems is often a feeling that something is desperately wrong, or that something is desperately right, and out of one or the other of these emergencies, something must be said (which leads to the rant or elegy about the desperately wrong thing or to the ode or love poem about the desperately right thing).

My specific context, of being of European descent, and from a working class family, female, and a local yokel citizen of the United States, led me to the extremes of these feelings, to both poles. It was mostly that by the time I was in elementary school I knew that something was desperately wrong on the local temporal level of what I'll call God and Country and Shopping Mall and then simultaneously that something was desperately right on an eternal level—that there was an order somewhere around me in nature that was both unifying and liberating, which is what I would later come to find expressed by Melville and Whitehead.

In my earnest romanticism, I'm curious about whether or not there was something particular about my visceral response to these feelings of wrongness and rightness and my need to vocalize them through writing. Which is to say I wonder whether or not poetry is a call. I've heard call stories and testimonies in religious communities, and they all share a similar framework—the "something-happened-to-me" framework of "one day I was walking down the street and I saw a cross or I saw a church, or someone called me 'Reverend,'" and so on and so forth.

In the circles I swing in as a poet, the call story often starts with Allen Ginsberg, as in, "I once was lost, but then I found Allen Ginsberg's 'Howl.'" (And it was a surprise to me and a little bit of a disappointment to learn that I was not the only one being called into poetry by "Howl" during my senior year of high school, and that in fact one of my other early heroes, Ed Sanders, had had that same experience in his senior year of high school in Missouri nearly thirty years before I did, and that many of my subsequent poetry students had the same experience in their senior years of high school decades later in places like New Jersey and Iowa and Ohio.) So I'll begin there because it's my story, and it's also my community's story.

When I was in my midteens, I spent a lot of time playing a tennis racket air guitar in my brother's bedroom (which held the shrine of the turntable) and listening to records that we'd managed to pick up at the department store down on Route 5. It was an accident (or incident) (or "flash of novelty" as Alfred North Whitehead might call it) around my air guitar jam sessions that tipped me off to the constellation of prophetic voices that included Allen Ginsberg. And it began when I came across an elegy called "Ballad of Hollis Brown" in which the author, Bob Dylan, at the age of twenty-two, pinned down a picture of the something-that-is-desperately-wrong. And I remember seeing Dylan perform that ballad on television in 1984 or 1985, with his typical hard-to-follow phrasings that caused one of my family members to blurt out, "Well, that was really terrible." But somehow I had absorbed, if not every word of it, every ounce of the pathos of it. The song is not based in historical fact; it's a story about a farmer in South Dakota who is starving and, in desperation, he loads his shotgun, blows out the brains of his wife and five children, and then kills himself.

And I found myself running off to my room to make notes about how incredibly transcendent it had been to hear this, how viscerally moved I was, at which point I think I really felt deeply that poetry, on the level that Dylan was presenting it, as a prophetic art, was a matter of life and death, and also that I was not going to be able to turn away from participating in it. I want to define what I mean by a "prophetic art," because I think that phrase can feel unapproachable, and it can definitely be misunderstood as some kind of hocus pocus that involves crystal balls. My definition of a prophetic art is informed by the writings of Old Testament scholar and theologian Walter Brueggemann. A prophetic art is an art that points out a difficulty in a present moment, relates it to a previous failing within a social contract (or covenant), and gives the listener options for potentially good or bad outcomes. Another way to say this is that a prophetic art is one in which the prophet is attuned to a higher order of things (some people might call it God, and some people might call it ethics or common decency). Spinoza makes it simple, defining a prophet as "one who interprets the revelations of God" and adding that "the power of prophecy implies not a peculiarly perfect mind, but a peculiarly vivid imagination."

I'll bring Walter Brueggemann's words directly into the conversation, as he's so brilliant a writer, and so immediately touched by the prophetic tradition in America through his friendship with Martin Luther King Jr. At the age of eighty-seven, he is one of the clearest prophetic voices in the wilderness of our global fascist neo-liberal late capitalist climate collapse. He writes, in a recent book, *The Practice of Prophetic Imagination*:

> It is the work of twenty-first century prophetic preachers . . . to name the denial and to identify the infidelities that make our common life toxic. It is the work of twenty-first century prophetic preachers . . . to name the despair and witness to the divine resolve for newness that may break the vicious cycle of self-destruction and make new common life possible.

What was haunting about the Bob Dylan ballad was the acknowledgment of that despair embedded in the American landscape, and implied in that was the despair of what Brueggemann identifies as democratic capitalism and militant consumerism (and in back of that, yes, the doctrine of discovery, colonialism, and slavery—which for me as a white teenager were the more invisible parts of the problem). Dylan's ballad reminded me that through an ethos of American individualism, some people are going to perish and some people are going to thrive and, for the most part, few people are going to say a word about it, and even fewer people are going to act to change things.

I still feel haunted in the same way by the opening of the second section of Ginsberg's "Howl," the Moloch section:

5

What sphinx of cement and aluminum bashed open their skulls and ate up
their brains and imagination?

Moloch! Solitude! Filth! Ugliness! Ashcans and unobtainable dollars!
Children screaming under the stairways! Boys sobbing in armies! Old
men weeping in the parks!

Moloch! Moloch! Nightmare of Moloch! Moloch the loveless! Mental
Moloch! Moloch the heavy judger of men!

Moloch the incomprehensible prison! Moloch the crossbone soulless
jailhouse and Congress of sorrows! Moloch whose buildings are
judgment! Moloch the vast stone of war!

THREE

I'm writing here in this lecture about how certain white men and certain
tales of white whales and a certain Whiteheadian cosmology gave me the
sustenance to begin to abandon Moloch, and how I learned from them
to begin to conspire with others who suffered, even when my efforts were
imperfect. I've been trying to trace that beautiful trajectory through my
early notebooks, from hearing Bob Dylan sing "Ballad of Hollis Brown"
to reading Allen Ginsberg's liner notes for Bob Dylan's album *Desire* and
then discovering Allen's poems, and then Jack Kerouac's work, and then
Alan Watts's *The Way of Zen*, and then Abbie Hoffman's *Revolution for
the Hell of It*, and then a few years later coming to the poet Robert Dun-
can, and the novelist Herman Melville, and the philosopher Alfred
North Whitehead, and so on, which, as you can see, is a big, steaming
pile of white men.

Their white maleness rarely appalled me (though Kerouac's later
would) because I saw the intentions they were setting in their various
poetics of liberation. Dylan's content on race told me something that no

6

one had ever explained to me at school about what it means to be Black and/or poor within the system, and subsequently what it means to be white and privileged within the system. (And not only had my community not revealed a truthful narrative, they had upheld racism at every turn.) Dylan was a white man in my poetical lineage, but he simultaneously was the first example for me of what a white co-conspirator might look like with his ballads about Medgar Evers and Hattie Carroll and Rubin Carter and Davey Moore and George Jackson, and with his insistence that America had no future because, as he said in an interview more recently, "it's a country founded on the backs of slaves."

I can go back to one of those first spiral notebooks and find my very reverent pencil-written transcriptions of Kerouac's and Ginsberg's ideas—Kerouac in *The Dharma Bums* saying: "I didn't feel that I was an American at all . . . my karma was to be born in America where nobody has any fun or believes in anything, especially freedom," and Ginsberg in his journals from the early 1950s embracing a really multifaceted inclusive queerness, as candidly and earnestly as ever:

At 14 I was an introvert, an atheist, a Communist and a Jew, and I still wanted to be president of the United States.

At 19, being no longer a virgin, I was a cocksucker, and believed in a supreme reality, an anarchist, a hipster totally apolitical Reichian; I wanted to be a great poet instead.

At 22 I was a hallucinating mystic believing in the City of God and I wanted to be a saint.

For me, they were the Ishmaels of *Moby-Dick* and not the Ahabs. They weren't the ones steering the ship; they didn't want to. They were the ones waking up in the arms of communists, Jews, anarchists, and even cannibals(!), happily, and going to sea to read the signs of the heavens. Even later when I came to Ezra Pound's poetry it was clear that, mad as he was, there had been something he had been searching for through the form of the poem that was meant to open the possibilities for how we see the world rather than to close it. Hearing testimonies from the first generation influenced by him, from Robert Duncan and from the film-maker Stan Brakhage and from the poet Jackson Mac Low, about the ecstasy of coming to *The Cantos*, is a clue in itself. That someone as queer as Duncan and someone as much of a misfit as Brakhage and someone of Jewish heritage as Mac Low was could all cleave to that work and could all be powerfully informed and transformed by it told me there was something in it besides fascist dogma.

FOUR

There was an agony involved in having deep feelings about the fact that something was very wrong but not having anyone else within a community to mirror that back to me. I find scrawled in one of my notebooks, December 22, 1986, a passage of Allen Ginsberg's from an unidentified text where he describes the challenge of "knowing how to feel human and holy and not like a madman in a world which is rigid and material-istic." There was also something agonizing about having prophetic creative energy alongside very primitive creative skills and a great distrust for any curriculum other than the liner notes of a Bob Dylan album.

It was that sort of agitation that drove Ishmael to ship out on the *Pequod*:

> Whenever I find myself growing grim about the mouth; whenever it is a
> damp, drizzly November in my soul; whenever I find myself involuntarily

pausing before coffin warehouses, and bringing up the rear of every funeral I meet; and especially whenever my hypos get such an upper hand of me, that it requires a strong moral principle to prevent me from deliberately stepping into the street, and methodically knocking people's hats off—then, I account it high time to get to sea as soon as I can.

I went to sea in a way I didn't expect to, and my *Pequod* was a community within the University at Buffalo, a small band of Ishmaels working for Ahabs. The most important of these Ishmaels for me were two white male poets, Robert Creeley and John (or Jack) Clarke. They were both in the English Department, though I don't think that either of them felt that they particularly belonged there, and they were both disheveled in the way that Ishmael's shipmates were in *Moby-Dick*. Bob had lost an eye as the result of a car accident and as a young person had happily traded in a plastic eyeball for an off-kilter squint, and Jack had had polio, so he hobbled through the hallway swinging his briefcase with a funny, steady determination. They were both heirs to that experimental American tradition that I mentioned at the beginning of this talk. Bob was a New Englander, a Harvard dropout, a poet of the lineage and stature of Dickinson and Williams. I guess I'd have to describe Jack as a Midwestern polymath. In addition to being a poet he was a jazz musician and Blake scholar and in his first years on the faculty at Buffalo he had met the poet Charles Olson and they became fast friends.

Neither Bob nor Jack were mentors in any conventional sense. Bob was at his best with people as a friend, and he always craved what he would call a "down-home" sociality. He had very little interest in assuming any mantle of authority. Jack was definitely something other than a college professor, though he hid it well under his tweed jacket and owl-like glasses and goatee.

I know when the tide turned for me exactly, when I realized that I could "get something" out of the academy on an afternoon as I listened to Jack enter into a conversation with a student, one of those Long Island football jocks, and Jack suggested that he might understand the reading material (Hesiod) better if he took psychedelic mushrooms. It was about week three into that class that I surrendered to his influence and scrawled in my notebook, "I love Odysseus." (Which makes me think of a time I was standing outside Riverside Church with one of my fellow seminary students and she blurted out: "I know King David was a whoremonger, but I love him anyway.")

As for Bob Creeley, I remember working up the courage to introduce myself to him on my first day of classes and saying, "I'm going to sign up for a poetry writing workshop and write poems!" and he was really opposed to that idea of entering into a contract to learn how to turn out poems as products. He had either declined to or had been not invited to teach such classes himself. In a gentle, brotherly way he suggested that perhaps if I wanted to be a poet I could study languages and history.

What I learned quickly about Jack and Bob is that they were thoroughly disinterested in poetry as a commodity, and they were disinterested in forcing poems into existence. Simultaneously, they were entirely committed to breaking down and maneuvering around any form (prosodic, academic, social) that restricted freedom, which is why I'm so willing to configure them using our contemporary cultural jargon as "allies." If a straightlaced poet like Robert Frost or anyone out of the line of the New Critics was mentioned in conversation, Bob and Jack would simply fume about the travesty of their tedious closed systems, a sentiment which put them at odds with most of the rest of the English Department. To return to my earnest romanticism, they confirmed what I suspected, that the retreat of the poem into academic institutions was the death of the prophetic tradition. I remember a young, very slick poet coming through town one autumn and Jack and Bob deliberating with each other about his work and Jack chewing on his lip and wrinkling his brow and saying, "Well, he could go either way." I still carry that with me, to a fault sometimes, because I do have friends who can stomach certain kinds of poems and poets and I think to myself if you want something like that you'd do just as well to go to Pottery Barn and look at the furniture.

In the same way that Bob Dylan and Allen Ginsberg had employed an earnest prophetic *content*, the writers I came to know through Bob and Jack employed an earnest prophetic *form*. They gave me an understanding that received systems are meant to be interrogated, opened, and rearranged. They showed me a world on the page that in no way resembled what I had seen in respectable literature anthologies. To break with a poetic formalism implied breaking with acceptable social behavior and acceptable social alliances. It meant crossing color lines. Bob's "rhythm" as a poet came not just out of William Carlos Williams, but also out of Max Roach. The prophetic tendency was often subtle in the content of Bob's work, but not always. I think of his poem "America":

> America, you ode for reality!
> Give back the people you took.
>
> Let the sun shine again
> on the four corners of the world
>
> you thought of first but do not
> own, or keep like a convenience.
>
> *People* are your own word, you
> invented that locus and term.

Here, you said and say, is
where we are. Give back

what we are, these people you made,
us, and nowhere but you to be.

William Blake's etching plates and Whitman's barbaric yawping stanzas
and Olson and Robert Duncan's field theory all prophetically rebelled
against what-was-wrong-with-the-world.

Duncan habitually explained this in his poems—his anarchist disdain
for polite order and his love affair with the idea that creative work had a
life force that made it a living part of the universe. It took me a long time
to understand that what he was writing about in his first full-length col-
lection, *The Opening of the Field*, is the same thing that Walter Bruegge-
mann is talking about when he describes a prophetic ministry as one that
upends the question of right- or left-wing politics. Duncan flat-out re-
jects what he calls "man-made" laws (including the Constitution of the
United States), seeking a "Law" with a capital *L*, an evolving order of
the universe absolutely aligned with Alfred North Whitehead's thinking.
"The Law I Love Is Major Mover" is a poem written in the midst of his
obsession with *Process and Reality*:

> Hear! Beautiful damnd man that lays down his law lays down
>   himself creates hell
> a sentence unfolding healthy heaven.
>
>   Thou wilt not allow the suns to move
>   nor man to mean desire move,
> . . . .
> Look!   the Angel that made a man of Jacob
>   made Israël in His embrace

was the Law,   was Syntax.

Him I love is major mover.

That major mover, that prime mover, that eternal Law, actually doesn't belong to the church (though Duncan's integration of Judeo-Christian myth here may give the false sense of such an alignment) and it doesn't belong to the state. There's a touch of Spinoza here, who in his *Theo-logico-Political Treatise* makes the same distinction between human law and divine law, dismissing human law as "a plan of living which serves only to render . . . the state secure." (One can't help but think of former Attorney General Bill Barr declaring genteel and gentrified New York City an "anarchist jurisdiction.")

Duncan's major mover, his God, is glimpsed through the creative processes of the poem and of the universe. There's something that the poet Don Byrd told me when I was writing the Duncan biography, about a reading Duncan gave of his *Passages* poems in Kansas in 1969. This would have been one of the readings where Duncan fully denounced what he saw as a literal satanism in the American occupation of Vietnam. Byrd said, "Somewhere in the midst of the apocalyptic passages, he stopped and said, 'Sometimes people ask me why, if I believe this, I bother to write poetry. I write poetry for the fucking stars.'"

FIVE

I had come to Duncan's prophetic anarchist imagination through a grad-uate seminar that Bob Creeley taught in the autumn of 1987. He was in-terested in reading deeply through the works of three of his contempo-raries, Duncan, Charles Olson, and John Ashbery. I didn't really know any of that work, so I said, "Can I sit in on that class?" And he said,

"Sure." This was a wild space when it comes to the theme of white men, a weekly three-hour seminar with about a dozen graduate students, all guys, who seemed very "mature" to me, though a number of them must have been in their midtwenties. And the guys always brought cigarettes for Bob, who wasn't really supposed to smoke anymore, and the more he smoked, the more personal he got in relating the poems to the friendships he had with Olson and Duncan, and it was all a little bit bawdy, but what I also remember about it is that Bob was insistent on maintaining a space for me in that company, and in creating a narrative for me (and hopefully especially for all the guys) about frankly what was wrong with patriarchal thinking (particularly Olson's) even as he was speaking about very dear friendships and very great poems.

My first real hearing of Duncan's work was there, with Bob reciting an early collage composition of Duncan's called "The Venice Poem" from 1947. If you know it, you know it is ornate and dramatic and queer, which was not what Bob was at all. He didn't do anything with the poem except to read it and to pause here and there and to say, "This is gorgeous, you dig?" And I really did "dig" but I had no idea why. I just knew that there were so many recesses and hiding places in the poem, that it was the kind of thing that my mother would have heard and said, "He thinks too much," and it was doing things that no poem was supposed to do.

In the same way that Allen Ginsberg had said things in the poem that no one was allowed to say, Duncan was doing things in the form of the poem that no one was allowed to do: he was creating an atmosphere and a world out of a collage of very disparate materials that included notes from a medieval history course he'd taken at Berkeley with Ernst Kantorowicz, and lines from Stravinsky's *Poetics of Music in the Form of Six Lessons*, and a long description of Henri Rousseau's painting "The

Dream," and excruciatingly personal journal entries about the end of a relationship including a climactic moment where he outs himself as a "cocksucker," which would have repercussions for him in his early publishing career.

It was really a very similar feeling to the one I'd had in hearing Dylan's "Ballad of Hollis Brown" for the first time. I knew Duncan had begun a conversation that was not allowed for in the world I inhabited. But again, it was more than that. It gave me a feeling of awe, and a feeling that a lot of people had been hiding this good stuff from me because it endangered the numbness of the culture.

SIX

I mentioned something at the beginning of this talk about waking up in the arms of cannibals and short-circuiting the power of the Ahabs steering the ships. If you've read *Moby-Dick*, you know the cannibal that Ishmael shares a bed with is named Queequeg and that Queequeg arrives at the beginning of the novel to figuratively penetrate Ishmael. Queequeg is the "dark-skinned cannibal" that the Roman historians saw in the dark-skinned Palestinian Jesus with his cult of body and blood. Ishmael says from their "bridal chamber" (as he calls it) in the Spouter-Inn:

> I began to be sensible of strange feelings. I felt a melting in me. No more my splintered heart and maddened hand were turned against the wolfish world. This soothing savage had redeemed it. There he sat, his very indifference speaking a nature in which there lurked no civilized hypocrisies and bland deceits.... I began to feel myself mysteriously drawn towards him.... I'll try a pagan friend, thought I, since Christian kindness has proved but hollow courtesy.

It's a sublime connectedness, a sublime co-conspiracy that Ishmael and Queequeg come into in that moment. It seems to me that every time I've come to something sublime in my life it's been accompanied by a feeling of being totally out of my depth, out of control, and it's often a sign that there are incredibly generative but also dangerously heated forces at work. This was the case for me with poetry, as it is with Christianity, which seem, for me, to be two calls linked in continuity, as part of one continuum. In the Duncanian line of thinking, such strange feelings and meltings, as Ishmael describes them, are a sure sign that Gnosis is active as a presence, and Gnosis is as wild as Eros, and in my experience they have often been collaborators.

The other part of my life at the university that autumn was a job I'd stumbled into in the rare books collection of the library system, which was exactly the place where Gnosis and Eros were running amok. The Ahab-like curator of the collection happened to be a scholar of Robert Duncan's poetry. Duncan was then sixty-eight and terminally ill with kidney and heart disease, and the curator had made a number of trips to San Francisco that year to bring back a very big fish, which was the whole of Duncan's manuscripts, notebooks, and library.

I think I must have leapt into the arms of the curator on that Tuesday afternoon in September after leaving Bob Creeley's lecture on "The Venice Poem," knowing that he could tell me more about the secrets hidden in the recesses of that work. My enthusiasm helped to forge an uneasy and very charged mentor-mentee relationship, but it also opened a literal door for me into what we called "the stacks," which was where all the manuscript materials were held, including Duncan's. No one was really allowed access to those papers; I soon learned they were definitely being kept out of the hands of visiting scholars, and they were definitely being treated as a commodity to be hoarded away until the curator had time to have his way with them. At some point that fall I struck a deal that since I was a lowly undergraduate student, and a girl, and of little threat to scholarly researchers doing real scholarly work, I was the perfect candidate to catalogue that collection. And so I did, every morning at 8:30 a.m., rushing into the office of the archives and sharpening my pencils and standing in front of rows of gray archival boxes filled with Duncan's eighty-one notebooks and feeling like that gnosis-gatherer Psyche did when she turned her lantern toward Eros.

If you know Duncan, you also know that he was proudly a San Franciscan, and that his work is infused with textures of the Bay Area and its Pacific shoreline, and so too were his notebooks. Opening those boxes unleashed the smell of the eucalyptus and rotting paper and fog dampness that settled in the alleys between the old Victorian houses in the Mission District. Eventually I read every page of every notebook and, as a courtesy to the curator, I created an index of what was on every page of every notebook, which began to look like a map of Robert Duncan's mind. I say that library was a place where Gnosis and Eros ran amok in that once I was wounded by that arrow, there was no other place I could happily be. I know this sounds familiar to the Duncanites in the audience because it is a variation of the testimony that Duncan gives about his own gnosis-crush facilitated by his high school English teacher Edna Keough, who brought him into a poetics through her love (and subsequently his love) for the Modernist poet H.D.'s work.

SEVEN

What I learned through being in that threesome with the Ahab-like curator and the big fish of Robert Duncan is that the only thing that couldn't be taken away from me in the instability of the temporal world was my relationship to those eternal orders of Gnosis and Eros and the Prophetic Creative Imagination. All of it led me away from the tedium of the Reagan-era warmongering pseudo-democratic capitalism that had swallowed up my adolescence. It makes me think of a poem of my own that was written around 1999 or 2000, and which I now see is really inflected with Duncan and Jack Clarke's influence in turning me toward a Homeric landscape. It's a song sung by Achilles, and it's called "Future Poem":

> Straight out of the Abraham Lincoln place
> in the middle of a primary election year
> which is snow inside the mind outside
> the tree and on the screen and if I were
> a cat I would scratch my ears
> all day and wear a woolen shirt
> and have a mate named Jimmy
> and we'd float away in a beautiful
> pea green boat that is just a dream,
> like the old people say
> out in their old poems out in the field
> and we are busy up outside inside
> our dreamscape with our boats,
> don't bother me, Agamemnon,
> I am busy with my boat.

Staying busy with an eternal boat is exactly what I'm doing when I'm in the poem. Duncan tuned my mind to the fact that humans are transcendent creatures when we manage to find the way there, or "the kingdom within" as Jesus calls it (to bring my own mythic tradition into the mix for a moment). Here is a quote from one of those eighty-one notebooks of Duncan's, this one from 1957 (exactly at the point that *Process and Reality* had entered his reading list): "our fate, our boundaries, are only the boundaries of the imagination through which the creative forces move."

What I had intuited about the potentialities of the poem were confirmed by Duncan and his circles (both at Black Mountain and in San Francisco): that a poem was obviously not a static commodity, it was an organic system living in time and space. It was Charles Olson who had discovered that within Alfred North Whitehead's *Process and Reality* cosmology were all the metaphors for how the poem worked in this fashion—as a novel process of revelation rather than as a product maintaining status quo boundaries on the page, such as evoked by Frost's neat quatrains and end rhyme and mending walls.

Whitehead, a British mathematician-philosopher with serious theological concerns, had originally presented the ideas of the book as an offering for the Gifford Lectures in Scotland in 1927–1928. The poetical cadences of his sentences, his quirky vocabulary, and his sympathy for Einstein's and Minkowski's revolutionary ideas about the nature of space and time, "the new science," as he called it, made him a perfect bedfellow for the poets (from Olson to Duncan to Ted Berrigan) who all poached from his ideas to bring a prophetic practice of poetry into the twentieth century.

I had to go back to the Duncan biography to remember the exact moment that *Process and Reality* descended on the American poetry scene.

It was in February of 1957, when Duncan invited Charles Olson to read at the San Francisco Poetry Center, and Olson arrived intoxicated on, perhaps among other things, Whitehead. Here is how the biography tells it:

> Olson infused the Bay Area scene with a new source of inspiration, giving a series of talks derived from "The Special View of History" lectures he had offered at Black Mountain the previous year. His presentations, given in Duncan and Jess's living room, overflowed with references to . . . *Process and Reality*, and his audience consisted of two dozen inquisitive young writers, including Michael McClure, Jack Spicer, Philip Whalen, and Michael Rumaker. Olson's reading of Whitehead seemed haphazard to some audience members, but the lectures consumed Duncan's imagination. The proposal that key themes in *Process and Reality* might be integrated into a poetics held great appeal. . . . Duncan's enthusiasm was well evident when he wrote to Robin Blaser later that year: "The great thing in music for the year has been the complete Webern . . . And one such book— Whitehead's *Process and Reality* that gives that grandeur. . . . It sets up a craving in me for large spatial architectures at the edge of the chaos. . . . My mind does not grasp it; my mind is graspd by it."

I think that all the poets, myself included, skipped over the systematic reading of Whitehead and immersed ourselves haphazardly in the texture of *Process and Reality*, which was really like stepping onto the *Pequod* and being cast out to sea. It wasn't to know it on an academic level, but to know it in the way that people "know" each other in the Bible, to have intercourse with it. It makes me think again of the divine abyss of *Moby-Dick*. Ishmael's shipmate Pip falls off the boat and goes mad in the experience of entering the depths:

The sea had jeeringly kept his finite body up, but drowned the infinite of his soul. Not drowned entirely, though. Rather carried down alive to wondrous depths, where strange shapes of the unwarped primal world glided to and fro before his passive eyes; and the miser-merman, Wisdom, revealed his hoarded heaps; and among the joyous, heartless, ever-juvenile eternities, Pip saw the multitudinous, God-omnipresent, coral insects, that out of the firmament of waters heaved the colossal orbs. He saw God's foot upon the treadle of the loom, and spoke it; and therefore his shipmates called him mad.

As an aside, I think of some occasions of seeing Stan Brakhage's films at his salons in Boulder, and of the great confusion his work caused to newcomers in the audience: that there were gaps, silences, long reelings of white space in the midst of his compositions. A whisper would go through the audience that something must be wrong with the projector when in fact Stan had simply made a film that reflected how the universe had presented itself to him. (As it had been with another Black Mountain associate, John Cage, and as it would be in the poems of Duncan and Olson, where pauses in the breath or quickenings of the heartbeat were entirely registered in the dance of the white space on the page with the projective typography and the presences evoked through phonetic resonances of the Logos.)

That too was inflected with a drive, as Whitehead would say, to embrace "the ultimate vibratory characters of organisms and . . . the potential element in nature."

EIGHT

It's funny to see now how my lifelong poetical influences congealed in a single season of the autumn of 1987. Three days a week I spent my mornings and late afternoons reading Duncan's notebooks, with an interlude between for Jack Clarke's Homer class. Every Tuesday was a full day with Bob Creeley: a morning undergraduate introduction to American poetry followed by watching him eat his lunch and drink from his thermos during his office hours, followed by his afternoon graduate seminar. What was it like to be schooled by those white men? The answer is that it was really just fine, even when it was less than perfect. Everything within those conversations about the poem prepared me to question my own embedded forms, my assumptions about language, my whiteness, and my privilege. Even when the mentors around me were imperfect, like King David the whoremonger, they had their ears open to how organisms danced in relation to the dance partners in their environment, how humans conspire against principalities, and how, as Duncan said brilliantly, "Responsibility is to keep the ability to respond." They encouraged my earnestness. I go to the Old English roots of that word *earnest* to find shadows of anger and ardour and desire and passion, all words that I associate with the prophetic tradition, that recall poetry's true value in its ability to challenge the oppressions that rise up in human systems, in what Walter Brueggemann calls "the Solomonic consciousness" when he conjures the image of King Solomon enslaving his own people to build the temple (or the White House, or the border wall).

You don't have to be involved in the Judeo-Christian tradition to see the desperate uprising of the royal consciousness in our lives today. And in the same way that a prophetic poetry develops through an accrual of tradition, I often have the feeling that the poets themselves (the actual entities, as Whitehead might call them) constellate together to show the outline of a "Law"—an inherent order of the universe. The continuity of the prophets is also an organic revelation of the universe's secrets. I want to close with a passage from *Process and Reality* that I found transcribed in one of Robert Duncan's reading notebooks around Whitehead:

> Each actual occasion contributes to the circumstances of its origin additional formative elements deepening its own peculiar individuality.

I hope that what I've said here helps to clarify the circumstances of my origin and the factors that shaped my own peculiar individuality as a poet. But I also hope it's clear, in the spirit of the thinking of these white men, and this tale of a white whale, and this Whiteheadian cosmology, that this story while indicative of some individual talent is also part of a larger phenomenon that is the prophetic imagination as it moves through history.

ABANDON THE
CREEPING MEATBALL

AN ANARCHO-SPIRITUAL TREATISE

I'd like to create some spaciousness in this talk. I'd like to think of it as an opportunity to peer into some rooms that are for me essential to my life as a poet. I'll call these rooms sacred places, and I will create a definition for the sacred which maybe will keep people from running away from it. I'll define the sacred for our purposes tonight as the impulses that connect us to life, the impulses that connect us to communities, human and creaturely communities. And I'll define the sacred also as the impulse that connects us to ancestors. The title of this talk is borrowed from Abbie Hoffman and Jerry Rubin and the Yippie Manifesto of 1968. But it's also inspired by a dialogue I had with the audience during my first lecture in this series. I want to particularly thank two friends who directed me out of lecture one and into lecture two. First, Joseph Gaglione, whom I've been talking to throughout this process and who made a really simple comment after the talk I gave back in November at Harvard. He said, "I liked it when you said people work too much," so I'm going to continue having that conversation here. And also I want to thank my friend Sarah Sohn, who suggested that I might want to wonder about the creative potential of being in a pickle, of being in a tight place.

That was her phrase, "being in a tight place." So what we might want to wonder about tonight are the generative things that can happen when we find ourselves in tight spots. Because we're going to be moving through a series of rooms here and I'm working with this theme of architecture, maybe we can imagine creative resistance as a series of secret passages around the margins of the dominant culture, around the margins of the things that feel suffocating to us. I think all of the rooms described in this talk are those secret passages.

Beginning with my friend Joseph's prompt, and the advice of the Yippies to "rise up and abandon the creeping meatball," I am going to also resist framing what I do as a poet as "work." Let's try to get rid of that from the beginning. Let's just get rid of any talk about poetry and careers altogether. In that, I'll invoke Louis Zukofsky and his line "The words are my life." I want to imagine in this space not a way of "working," but a way of living: a way of resistance to that which doesn't give life and a way of being open to the revelations that do connect us to life and to others. So I'm going to hold two ideas in mind in relation to the subtitle of this talk: the "anarcho-spiritual" part of it. Let's talk about creative practices that resist "accomplishment," and let's talk about creative practices that in their resistance reveal the world in a new light.

The first room is not just a room but also a book. The room is in a house on the north side of Buffalo in the late 1980s. The book is *The H.D. Book* by Robert Duncan. The house, at 67 Englewood Avenue, housed an anarchist collective, or at least we, the inhabitants, imagined ourselves that way. There were usually about ten of us living in that house at a time, in our late teens and early twenties, mostly students. I've been trying to remember what drew us all together there. Our scene was a little bit queer, it was very much to the left of center, and I think we were mostly coming from tight places, economically, within our families of origin. We were mostly of the first generation in our families to go to college. Two instincts were very alive in that moment, in that house: first, a fierce resistance to the culture around us; to the educational culture, to the social expectations, to the state, to religion. And we did identify as anarchists with a capital *A*: we were very clear that anarchy never meant "helter-skelter" chaos, but that it meant listening for more organic alternatives to the inscribed laws around us. We were looking for natural orders of community. And that resistance to the culture made room for a lot of revelation about potential alternatives.

In my room in that house there was a teapot, an orange and white cat, a typewriter, a record player, and a Lenny Bruce album that began with the skit "Lima, Ohio":

> I worked at a place called Lima, Ohio. . . . When you travel in these towns there's nothing to do during the day. . . . they're very boring. The first day you go through the five-and-ten. The next day you go to the park. You see the cannon and you've had it. . . . The lending library and the drugstore. Yeah, it doesn't make it.

It's funny to think I would find that album at all. It was released about 1962 and Lenny Bruce died a year before I was born. But what I responded to in that opening little skit on that album was that Lima, Ohio was a tight place. I know now that part of the reason I was steered toward a poetics of resistance and revelation is that I had come out of a similarly tight place. I was thinking about how in the south towns of Buffalo there were only so many places you could go, and only so many times you could swing on the clothing racks at the Hens & Kelly department store before you got terribly bored. I'm really thankful for it at this point, for my cow town of Derby, New York, and for the ancestral cow towns of my people on the outskirts of places like Ryńsk and Kraków. There's a mystery for me in the Polish Catholic great-grandparents who were literally from towns with cows, and then the grandparents who didn't go beyond an eighth-grade education and were working at the Bethlehem Steel Plant and working on the railroad lines around it and of course going to church every Sunday at Saint Joachim's and Saint Hyacinth's. So if you know Lenny Bruce, you know the rest of that album I was listening to was configured around this beautiful fantasy of the Pope as closet Jewish homosexual who oversees a Madison Avenue corporation called Religions, Inc. Between Lima, Ohio, and Religions, Inc., Lenny Bruce had described the prevailing winds of my whole childhood scene. He was halfway between my grandparents' generation and my parents' generation, and he was impatiently taking apart all aspects of their sacred culture, from the five-and-ten to the Church, which I obviously had my doubts about too. I don't think I would have become a poet without that tension in the double ancestral line: of coming from that tight place of the cow-town ancestors and then finding a way to revel in a critique of what ailed them via Lenny Bruce and Abbie Hoffman and others. Thank God for all of them, that they gave me the latitude to wander out of their little cow towns into the life that I have.

When I was putting together the manuscript for the book called *Black Dog Songs* with my editor at Flood Editions, Devin Johnston, we got around to the idea of looking at early poems that had never made it into a book, poems that were part of that initial moment of coming into a vocation. There's a little piece we included that ended up with the title "Triptych," three poems that seemed linked to each other that definitely were written in that room with the typewriter and the orange and white cat and the Lenny Bruce album. The first part of that triptych sequence really stands out to me now as the beginning of my own understanding of revelation in poetry. It was one of the first poems I think that I created simply by listening for and receiving material for the poem rather than trying to make something happen. I think now that this is where I became a poet "for real," when I stopped trying to "GO SOMEWHERE" (speaking of Manifest Destiny) with the poem and instead I let the poem occur:

> occurs a curve of
> sound or sign
>
> occurs a curve
> of sound design waiting
>
> awaiting occurs
> a curve of sound design

Well that was very different than what I had been doing early on in imitations of Beat poetry. Because that first instinct for me as a poet had been that I really wanted to SAY SOMETHING, DO SOMETHING, and GO SOMEWHERE! to get at the empathy I had for the world and to pour out my own feeling states. That's what at some point I started to describe to students as "the dead grandmother poem," the really urgent need to say something about one's personal experience that was sometimes not so interesting. When I look at this poem now, "occurs a curve of sound or sign" is a phrase that is really a good description of how my process as a poet works. Because usually what occurs first is a sound that might be a phrase lingering, from waking life, or from a dream, or possibly from something heard or misheard in a public space—a little piece of revelation. And other times that impulse for the poem is a sign that comes first: a shadow on a sidewalk, something neon, or a particular glow in a field from a train window. Light. And sometimes there's a nonspecific longing that sparks the poem: a waiting or awaiting, as the poem says, that sparks the first syllable of the event of the poem.

So I wondered in that moment in that room if this was in fact a "real" poem because it seemed to not be going anywhere or doing anything. It was not about what I was trying to make the poem say but about what the poem was trying to make me say. But I knew also that I was on the right track because of the place I had come to through being engaged in Robert Duncan's poetry and poetics. His was the first thinking I read about the spiritual mystery of poetry. And I'm again just going to invoke the sacred language here because at this point as a poet-pastor it's how my work is configured in my mind, and probably always was even when I was at my most secular atheistic. So, that thinking was fed by Robert Duncan's essays on poetics, collected in *Fictive Certainties*, published by New Directions in the mid-1980s, made up of talks Duncan had given around the country during the 1960s and 1970s where he was really at his peak of expounding on what a poetics was for him, and where he very clearly claimed poetry as a divine impulse. Duncan says, "Words send me," much like Zukofsky says, "The words are my life."

At that moment, among the poets I knew, there was a conversation going on about another book of Duncan's which was not yet a book, but was a rumor of a book, called *The H.D. Book*, and it was often spoken of as if it were a portal to another universe. It was a multidecade critical project that Duncan began writing in the early 1960s, through which he was going to tell the "secrets" he knew about Modernist poetry, occult practices, and the intersections of occult practices and poetry. He had titled it *The H.D. Book* as an homage to his poetical ancestral mother, the poet H.D., or Hilda Doolittle (1886–1961), whose work he had first encountered in high school in the 1930s. Duncan privately described the *The H.D. Book* as a tribute to the women in his life. It was a tribute to two ancestral lineages: to writers like H.D. and Gertrude Stein and Laura Riding and to the women in the family he had been adopted into: his mother, grandmother, and particularly his Aunt Faye who had been an ardent occultist and a devotee of the works of Shakespeare. Those of you who know Duncan know that he had been raised in a hermetic brotherhood, which was a little bit Rosicrucian, and a little bit wacky West Coast Masonic lodge culture from the turn of the century. But part of the attraction for him of H.D.'s work and person was that H.D. had been raised in the Moravian Church in Bethlehem, Pennsylvania. Her family was ancestrally spiritually connected to Count Zinzendorf who had founded the Moravian sect as a secret brotherhood. And part of the reason that I was so eager to get my hands on *The H.D. Book* manuscript is that Duncan claimed that in a meeting with H.D. she had revealed to him that while she was living in England during the Second World War she had been initiated into a Roman Mithras cult. That sounded very extraordinary to me, even though I didn't know then and still am not sure what a Roman Mithras cult is. Whatever *The H.D. Book* was, we poets suspected there was a reason that it hadn't seen the light of day, or at least had only circulated to a chosen few of Duncan's friends.

I knew where the many various threads of *The H.D. Book* manuscript were to be found, at the University at Buffalo's Poetry Collection, my place of employment. What makes the story all the more intriguing is the appearance in Buffalo at that time, somewhere around the spring of

1988, of a John the Baptist–like figure whose name was Harvey Brown. Harvey was in his early fifties when I met him. The urban myth of the tall, golden-locked, bronze-skinned Harvey Huntington Brown III was that he was a descendant of the abolitionist John Brown and that he was part of an inner (or at least outer) circle around Peter Tosh and Bob Marley whom he had met while running drugs from Jamaica to Belize in a canoe with a voodoo priestess. He was an old friend of my professor Jack Clarke, so the dodgy aspects of his story, which Jack neither confirmed nor denied, simply lingered in the air. The Jamaican reggae part of Harvey's life remains unconfirmed, but as for the John Brown lineage, that was not true. Harvey in fact came from a long line of Cleveland industrialists who had made their fortune around the steel industry on the Great Lakes, and he had come into an inheritance as a young person, courtesy of the Brown Hoisting and Conveying Machine Company of Cleveland, Ohio. He had had a long history by the time I met him of using his money to support poets including Charles Olson and John Wieners and to publish books of poetry and plays and fiction, great Americana works: Sherwood Anderson, William Carlos Williams, etc., that had either been overlooked, lapsed out of print, or in some cases had never been published. Harvey felt very strongly about these things, always with the thought that there was something at stake on a metaphysical level in bringing poetry to the light. Particularly a manuscript of poems of H.D.'s called *Hermetic Definition* fell into this category for Harvey. It was very clear that H.D.'s literary executor was holding some of her work from view, and in an act of resistance and revelation, Harvey smuggled the manuscript out of the Beinecke Library at Yale and published it as a very beautiful book in 1971 under his imprint Frontier Press.

The atmosphere around Harvey was so delightful. He was a thorn in the side of all progress-driven Ahabs. It turned out Harvey had his own ideas about *The H.D. Book,* one that intersected with mine (that it was a sacred text) and one that hadn't occurred to me (that it should be found, gathered, and published immediately). In Harvey's mind, that work was being kept out of view, again, by a literary executor. A little group of anarcho-spiritualist poets who already worked at the Poetry Collection eagerly volunteered to carry out a reconnaissance mission to dig through Duncan's then unsorted papers and liberate the various pieces of the manuscript from the library, chapter by chapter, to hand over to Harvey for publication as a Frontier Press book. Harvey was never able to publish it. He died of cancer two years later. But the bootleg version of *The H.D. Book* would circulate for another twenty-five years, first as a bound paper manuscript, then as a floppy disk that showed up mysteriously in my mailbox one day around 1993, then as an online offering, and finally as an official publication through the University of California Press, one of its co-editors having been a co-conspirator in the original bootlegging crew.

The H.D. Book became the single most important influence on my understanding of a poetics. And not a single page of it disappointed. It was a place where an ethos of poetry emerged that demanded both an openness to the potential forms of the universe and a rejection of the status quo. It was absolutely an anarcho-spiritual treatise of resistance and revelation. I keep thinking of Duncan's line in a miscellaneous lecture; I suspect it was at New College of California when he was in his last semester of teaching and was quite ill and was determined to pass down everything he knew about H.D.'s work. He said, "One-half of the world is looking for something nasty and one-half of the world is looking for something gnostic." The gnostic impulse at that moment in Buffalo in the 1980s held great sway. I think it gave us all a sense of belonging in that small, strange community of poet-seekers. It opened up the possibility of reclaiming texts from academia and academic discourse. Creative works were not commodities in an education racket and books of poems were not the property of literary executors or libraries. Harvey's message through his work with Frontier Press and Duncan's message in *The H.D. Book* were that there was a value in reclaiming sacred connections, communities, and ancestors, those nets and lines of association as Duncan called them. I learned not only to write poems through Duncan's influence but how to read texts: to find the interior light in a work. It was never about being able to understand and summarize; it was about being *sent* by the text. In the opening pages of *The H.D. Book* Duncan describes reading James Joyce with two female classmates out on the lawn of the campus at Berkeley. He writes:

> The poet . . . is a worker, for the language . . . belongs to the productive orders and means in which the communal good lies. All that is unjust, all that has been taken over for private exploitation from the commune, leaves us restless with time, divorced from the eternal. If I had come under the orders of poetry, I saw too that those orders would come into their full volition only when poetry was no longer taken to be a profession and when the poet would be seen to share in the daily labor toward the common need.

The second room is a poem and a house and a city. By the late spring of 1989 I was ready to leave Buffalo. My two favorite teachers suddenly became unavailable. Bob Creeley had gone to teach in Helsinki and Jack Clarke had been diagnosed with cancer and was rarely able to be in the classroom. Our anarchist collective had imploded. I had finished my work of cataloging Robert Duncan's papers at the Rare Books Collection, and *The H.D. Book* had been smuggled out of the library and was in Harvey Brown's hands. Being about a dozen credits short of a degree, I dropped out. I left Buffalo with two friends on a wild and woolly car trip across the country to San Francisco where we found an apartment on a tiny alley called Rose Street near Civic Center. There was never any question in my mind about where I thought I needed to be. I had no job prospects, few job skills and definitely no social skills, no money, but I needed to be in the city that Robert Duncan's poems had been written in. I had on two previous occasions visited San Francisco to be in the company of Robert Duncan's widow, the painter and collage artist Jess Collins, who lived in the house that they had shared in the Mission District of San Francisco for more than thirty years. Once I arrived, I didn't see Jess often. He and I were both miserably shy, but occasionally I gathered the nerve to call him and make a plan for lunch. I memorized the route from Market Street to the Mission. I memorized the visuals of the Spanish fish markets leading toward the house. I learned the differences between the angles of light on the East Coast and the West Coast by watching the glare of the sun against the boxes of oranges lined up on Valencia Street. I memorized the afternoon sounds coming out of the bars and storefront churches all through that neighborhood. I memorized the scent of plantains frying in butter. I knew the progression of cross streets on the way to the house: Mission Street, Capp Street, South Van Ness Avenue, Shotwell Street, Folsom Street. It was all useless knowledge, at least until I became Duncan's biographer. As for the big, looming Victorian house where Jess would greet me at the top of the stairs, peering out from behind what seemed like a massive Transylvanian castle door, that house was actually a sacred place. Firstly, Robert Duncan's books were there, and his trinkets, his record collection, his hats, his cape, even his kitchen spices. Part of every visit was the treat of Jess letting me wander through several rooms of libraries spread out across three floors, especially the first-floor library to the left of the living room where the hermetic, gnostic, theosophical, theological books were shelved. Let's peer into that room: there's an ornate desk with a small lamp, a stained glass lampshade, a telephone, an address book, the scraps of paper that Jess fetched to write notes for me of books to read and phone numbers of friends around town whom I might want to be in touch with. The feeling of being totally enveloped in the dark wood and towering shelves, and the books salvaged variously from Duncan's parents' library and from bookstores Duncan had regularly scoured during his reading tours. That room was for me a portal. It was a room where one might actually be transported. It was a room that as far as I was concerned could raise the dead. Stories were being told even in the lettering on the spines of the books: *Orpheus the Fisher* by Robert Eisler, *By Light, Light: The Mystic Gospel of Hellenistic Judaism* by E. R. Goodenough, *A Dictionary of Angels* by Gustav Davidson, *The Hidden Church of the Holy Graal* by A. E. Waite. The resources that had fed *The H.D. Book* were all there.

I associate that whim to cross the country and to be in that library with a poem of Duncan's from a series of derivations of Gertrude Stein's work that he wrote in the early 1950s. The book in fact was called *Derivations*. The poem is called "Turning Into":

> turning into a restful roomfull;
> turning into a guide to the book;

turning into a man-naked memory;
turning into a long avenue;
turning into a lady reclining;
turning into a mother declining;
turning into a vegetable declaiming;
turning into a yesterday for tomorrow;
turning into an age old sorrow;
turning into a cat fit for fiddling;
turning into a wheel withering;
turning into a god whose heart's at ease;
turning into an hour of sore dis-ease;
turning into an eagle bottle January;
turning into a hairy baby song;
turning into an all night long;
turning into a doctor's office;
turning into a rubber grimace;
turning into a snail's pace,
      a rail's distance, a long face;
turning into a turn with grace.

I was "turning into," peering into, breathing my way into the assemblage that was Duncan's house and Duncan's city. If I had had any conceit that my early "real" triptych poem had sprung from nowhere, I had overlooked that it had also sprung from the line of Stein and Duncan. Here is another piece of that triptych that began with "occurs a curve":

dwelling upon an instance,
dwelling upon an household, a dwelling
delving into a dwelling, an household
an absence.

an absence in a dwelling
dwelling upon a delving into an absence
in an household.

a silent absent dwelling upon a
delving into an instance of an absence
in a dwelling.

Duncan and Jess had been married in 1951. In 1967 they were able to purchase that house, that condemned dwelling in a neighborhood that was not yet the center of anything in San Francisco, having borrowed money from a friend. The house became a place of resistance much as their self-proclaimed marriage had been an act of resistance. The house was also meant to be a place of revelation as an architectural organism: a place where layers of old wallpaper could be peeled back into another era, and where tangled old electrical wires could be rerouted to create light. Duncan and Jess took a stand against the going reality which didn't suit them at all, but they did it not out of despair or anger; they did it with an insistence that there was an utterly joyful way to live that had nothing to do with money or what the expectations of their families or neighbors were. They lived off the grid, in their own special way. When I interviewed Michael McClure for the Duncan biography he gave the most beautiful picture of this, and of the way this ethos was passed down to a younger generation of poets:

They actually set the styles for us . . . their style of living and the community that grew from the earlier anarchist bohemian tradition. . . . We were all very poor. . . . watching Robert and Jess make the first bouillabaisse I'd ever seen . . . —to make such a thing was a big affair. I'd never dreamed that such a thing existed. . . . To watch them take a squid and put saffron into it and do all this, and you had a party with your friends. . . . There was great vigor and involvement in things. . . . what I'm calling poverty was actually very rich. Robert and Jess were living with less money than they actually had because much of what they had went into buying art from their friends.

That every activity within a household could be sacred was what the thirteenth-century Japanese monk Dōgen also knew: "When you prepare food, do not see with ordinary eyes and do not think with ordinary mind. Take up a blade of grass and construct a treasure king's land; enter into a particle of dust and turn the great dharma wheel." I can't help but think Duncan and Jess would have loved that. It's certainly what I felt when I sat at the kitchen table and watched Jess arrange plates of fried chicken liver and asparagus and delicate butter cookies. That too was an education. The other education was about "not working." Jess had abandoned the creeping meatball after a stint in the army during the Second World War. Trained as a chemist, he was put to work on the Manhattan Project. The bombing of Hiroshima had come on his twenty-second birthday. He stopped working and became a painter.

I'm trying to get at what I was looking for there, at Duncan and Jess's house, and what I found. The word Muse-um suits it: it was a space made hospitable for the appearance of the muses. What I found was not only a space for the imagination that ran counter to the dead feeling of a tight place like Lima, Ohio, but also a form of order and gentleness and absolute joy that didn't depend on any external social cue. Within that household was the creation of a hearth light in a very primal way. It was also a reminder that one didn't need to go anywhere, that PROGRESS was unnecessary. In our occasional afternoons together, sometimes walking down the street to a local taco place, Jess showed me what it could mean to live hyperlocally, to never need resources beyond the local fish market and local dumpsters and local Salvation Army where bits and pieces of a world of collage and assemblage material might be found.

Around the same time that I was experiencing that household, at the end of my first summer in San Francisco, a friend from our anarchist collective in Buffalo came through town and stayed with us on Rose Street. It was August of 1989. She said she wanted us to meet her dad, a still-life painter who was living in the East Bay in Oakland. There were about five of us who went out that night, across the block to the Lower Haight to a little bar called Noc Noc where we squeezed into a grungy, angular metallic booth. I remember it all now like an out-of-body experience: I can see the scene from across the room, or from the ceiling looking down. My friend's dad, Bruce Kurland, was at the center of the conversation. There was cigarette smoke issuing from his mouth as he talked, his salt-and-pepper hair disheveled, kind of punk, something sweet about the angle of his wrist as he flicked ashes across the table. His face lit up occasionally with an exclamation. He had a real excitement at being in company, in conversation, in community. He was relating his awe at a line from Melville's *Moby-Dick*. He said it more than once: "It was the whiteness of the whale that appalled me."

I'll read the original text of Melville's. It's a tiny bit different than Bruce remembered it. This is Ishmael speaking:

> What the White Whale was to Ahab, has been hinted; what, at times, he was to me, as yet remains unsaid.
>
> Aside from those more obvious considerations touching Moby Dick, which could not but occasionally awaken in any man's soul some alarm,

there was another thought, or rather vague, nameless horror concerning him, which at times by its intensity completely overpowered all the rest; and yet so mystical and well nigh ineffable was it, that I almost despair of putting it in a comprehensible form. It was the whiteness of the whale that above all things appalled me.

I think that describes the feeling I've had in writing this lecture. To use Melville's words, what is "mystical and well nigh ineffable" is what I've been trying to get at in this journey through these sacred rooms, a feeling state rather than a neat answer to what these mysteries are as they appear in our lives or as they appear on the horizon of the sea. It was the wonder in Bruce's voice that was infectious, so much so that I took my friend's words very literally when she said, "You're going to love my dad," because I really did, in what became a May–November romance and later a best-friendship. He had hooked me in that moment on something that was a mystery, in the same way that I had heard there was a mystery in *The H.D. Book*. I wanted to know what had gotten him so worked up about this scene in *Moby-Dick*. He obviously was not approaching any of this as an academic discourse on a great novel in American literature. Bruce, like Robert Duncan, was truly ungraduated and unanalyzed. *Moby-Dick* was something that he was taking quite personally. Around the edges of the world in that chase for that whale was an unknown that was big, appalling, terrifying, and could have repercussions for all of our lives. At least that is how it sounded when Bruce brought it up over beers that night. I later found out that he knew about the sea from adventures in the Coast Guard during his late teens. He had in fact been assigned to a cutter called the *Acushnet* which shared the name of the whaling ship Melville had worked on in 1841 that inspired the writing of *Moby-Dick*.

Bruce knew about the emptiness of the sea and the feeling of absolute terror at its vastness. He knew about the wonder that the natural world held. His fascination with that phrase about the whiteness of the whale was not a sociopolitical reading of Melville but rather a question posed from the perspective of a painter who painted nature and was always wrestling with what was elusive in the creaturely world, which Bruce was always launching himself into headfirst as he had as a kid out on the marshes of Long Island. He would argue fiercely that it was not a spiritual pursuit. But he kept looking for something. Melville was one place that he liked to excavate. Henry Miller's writing was another, then the paintings of Velázquez, and definitely the Dutch tradition of still-life painting.

I want to pry the door open a little bit and leave it ajar. We lived in a small, square, brick warehouse loft in a deserted strip of streets a couple blocks from the Oakland estuary and a couple of blocks from Oakland's Chinatown neighborhood, within earshot of the I-580 freeway overpass. If you look in you can see Bruce not at his easel (no one was ever allowed in his studio) but in a small, sparsely furnished side room whose only furniture was a single bed and a long shelf constructed of raw wood to hold three large freshwater fish tanks. The air was thick with the smell of linseed oil and industrial-strength French roast coffee heated and re-heated on the stove until only an acidic muddy residue was left on the bottom of the pot. He was younger than I am now, at least by a year or two. His khaki pants were paint-stained, his button-down shirt was like-wise streaked with paint, his sleeves were rolled up, a little bit thread-bare, his gaze fixed on a school of guppies, maybe a question about the placement of a filter or an aquatic plant, a Marlboro Light 100 dangling from his mouth. His hand was dancing in the air. He was absentmindedly conducting a paint symphony, always rehearsing a brushstroke that might capture a moment in nature: a magnolia opening, light streaming into its maw, a blue crab tumbling out of a bin at a sidewalk market down the street in Chinatown.

Always just beyond reach in the painting was a moment of ecstasy in nature—a moment of revelation of something simultaneously terrible and beautiful. And too he was conscious of what happened when humans stepped into the picture—a bird dangling from a string, game laid lifeless on a banquet table, conquered, the bald, white eyeball of a sheep's head, staring out from a box. The idea that I had toyed with in reading Abbie Hoffman, to "abandon the creeping meatball," was not something Bruce had had to think about, for better and for worse. He was single-mindedly devoted to spending his days painting his way into a world, into an intimacy with the things of nature. Often there was a pause in his breath—he was breathtaken by certain visuals—the skewered duck carcasses in the windows of the Chinese restaurants in downtown Oakland, the dance of the plovers and the lesser yellowlegs along the tide line at Point Reyes in Marin County. He knew the name of every bird, where it had flown in from, whether it was mating or not, and where it would fly out to again.

Hours of the morning could pass by with him wanting to talk, to ask me questions about what I knew about poetry. What were the technical specifications of a certain form? What was the history of one line of thought or another about the spiritual in poetry? About Modernism? About abstraction? He could build cosmologies over the course of a pot of coffee and a pack of cigarettes: of the relationships between the wing structure of a particular bird and the design of a B-17 airplane, of the reasons that a Japanese Zero fighter plane was superior to a German Messerschmitt. Of how something called the Venturi Principle explained the lift of the wing of a plane. I only recognized later how important these kinds of conversations were to Bruce's absolutely unschooled intellectual life and to the inspiration he took into the studio when he sat down at his easel to paint. As I had witnessed in my first meeting with him in the bar in the Lower Haight, he needed to be in company and talk through the books he'd devoured and the public television documentaries he had watched into the late hours of the night. At Bruce's memorial in the spring of 2014 in New York, his brother Jeffrey, an anthropology professor, said, "Bruce and I could talk about the Upper Paleolithic for hours." That was my Bruce too.

I don't think I wrote a single memorable poem during that time. I was too busy taking in what was happening around me. The poem that would be a narrative of that place came later when I moved to New York. It was written around 1996, and was a book-length sequence called *Sea Lyrics*, the title stolen from a Jack London book, as he too had lived in Oakland and wandered the estuary waterfront:

At dawn bent at odd angles the exercisers in the yard speaking only dialects of fog, there were fish and then tattoos, where we walked upon the waterfront of cave bluffs, where the waterfront held shrimp, where there were three dozen tourists behind the Thailand disco beat, where the ferry left at dawn, where the buses never came, where the sidewalk was all buckled, where the customs seemed all strange, where I walked in shadows of the eucalyptus night, where I seldom rode in cabs, where I never owned a blue and shiny truck, where you slowly bobbed your tea bag, where the apple trees turned black, where I washed the fish inside the fountain in the park, where I had been a long time in this story on the bridge, where I have been wearing avocados all day, where I am all tattoos and dreams of fashion, across the glare of the roof, near the church of Thelonious Monk, where I have seen the soot upon the windows of tattoos.

It still retains the Steinian-Duncanian repetition. That derivative impulse never left my work, but in its content it's totally inflected through the influence of Bruce's painting life and our life together in the shadow of the freeway overpass.

The absurd is there: the conflict between humans and nature, and what that looks like in an urban landscape. There was no illusion in Bruce's work that there was a perfection to come. He was conscious of the destructive forces all around him, of the Ahabs, of "the Art Pigs" as he called them—the galleries and art dealers and patrons whom he despised for stealing his time. Humans of that sort for him fell into the same category as those who had transformed the marshes of his childhood into industrial waste sites.

I'm curious about that trope of light as it comes into Bruce's paintings, and as it comes in as a metaphor for resistance and revelation. The word "light" has been on my mind throughout the writing of these passages. Bruce was sure that the light was not holy and that God had never existed. A few weeks ago, in the midst of thinking about this talk, I went to the Metropolitan Museum on a whim. I had the feeling there was something there for me to look at, if only for a moment, something to connect to in relation to this lecture. I suspected it was Monet, whose later work, the cataract-inflected water lily paintings, Bruce loved. I wanted to think about that light in Monet as a portal, to dispute Bruce's claim that God was dead. He would have totally disagreed with me. I wish I could have that conversation with him now, at the end of four years of seminary. He'd still win the argument, just out of his Taurean insistence that I was wrong, but he'd want to know all of the mental gymnastics carried out by the theologians around various issues from light to life to the flight of birds.

So I went to the museum to stand in front of *Haystacks (Effect of Snow and Sun)* maybe just to bask in its light, to think about the fact that the light painted by Monet is the same light that just keeps streaming through the world to humans, year after year, century after century. Even in those hayfields on the outskirts of Kraków where my great-grandparents stood. I'm going to end with a beautiful little passage of Robert Duncan's from a notebook, a draft of notes toward what would have been a third volume of *The H.D. Book,* where he draws this all together for me: the revelation, the sacredness of connection, the way we are derived from ancestors, and the double wonder of the spiritual and scientific instincts that we live inside of:

All our being is derivative . . . the true authenticity or authority of which lies hidden in the potentialities of the DNA code. Here Blake's *authors in eternity* are then in biological terms those as yet unrealized angelic potentialities who work in the chemical ground of the cosmos to realize what life is in the multitude of forms . . . All forms then participate in Form that has not yet completed itself but comes into being through them.

III

EPISTLE TO THE SUMMER
WRITING PROGRAM

(ON THE METAPHYSICS OF DEEP GOSSIP)

I want to tell you a story about the first summer that I lived in New York City which is a story that begins at the beginning of June in 1994 when I moved into a studio apartment on East 6th Street between Avenue A and Avenue B on the north side of the street a half block from the SideWalk Cafe where they had tables outside where you could drink tea and eat English muffins and it was also the summer of the O.J. Simpson white Bronco car chase which I watched on TV with my friend Dave who also moved to New York that summer and lived with me in the studio apartment on East 6th Street between Avenues A and B and I want to propose that it was a really hot and humid summer or at least that's how I remember it now, that there was a weird funky stench that I thought was cat pee but it was really the tree of heaven shoots growing in the little patches of green between the buildings like in the book *A Tree Grows in Brooklyn* which I've never read, and the garden level studio apartment was where Dave and I watched the O.J. Simpson white Bronco car chase on the TV and where there were a few pieces of furniture including a table and a refrigerator and a bed and probably a couple of chairs and Dave slept in the bed and I slept on the floor because we had made a deal that the first one who got a job could sleep in the bed and he got a job first working as a printer down in SoHo for his friend Henry's father which meant he had the right to the bed and I got a job second with the help of the dancer Sally Silvers whose dancing I loved because she reminded me of Charlie Chaplin but what I really remember is that the shower there in that apartment was a dingy pink color because it was also the summer with something on the news that they were calling "the flesh-eating virus" so every time I got in the shower and I noticed a scratch or a mosquito bite I thought I had the flesh-eating virus and that I was going to die and also one more detail is that when I slept on the pile of blankets on the linoleum floor which was my bed I was surrounded by roach families waving their antennae from the nooks and crannies of the baseboards with the cat pee smell of the tree of heaven trees coming from the ground-level windows that looked out over not much except the back of another building and this all felt like something new which is to say that it was disorienting to be in New York City which seemed really exotic to me and also to my friend Dave because we were from Buffalo where you have to work very hard to have something exciting happen on a summer afternoon but in New York it seemed like something exciting was happening every second of the day and even the subways and bodegas were open all night and the Chinese food restaurants also like the one on Avenue C and 9th Street where I preferred the roast pork and vegetables on rice which was downstairs from the building where we found out through the grapevine that a criminally insane cannibal had eaten his girlfriend in 1989 and two blocks away from the studio apartment shared by me and Dave and the roaches was Bernadette Mayer's apartment on East 4th Street that she shared with Phil who was her boyfriend and Marie and Sophia and Max who

47

were her children and also with a lot of roaches but with no other pets and the point is that I moved to New York City to have this experience, to live down the street from Bernadette but not necessarily to live near cannibals or roaches because all I ever wanted to do was to listen to Bernadette talk.

I want to tell you why all I ever wanted to do was to listen to Bernadette talk which was because she had a way of saying things that at first seemed like they were mundane but they were always transcendent and this included the way she asked questions that made you think more deeply about life like if you really had a crush on someone she would ask, "Is he your mother or your father?" so on almost every night after I spent the day in the bed which was a pile of blankets on the floor reading the *Village Voice* want ads because I was kind of looking for a job I would walk the two blocks down Avenue A past the Key Food supermarket and the couple of remaining tiny Polish storefronts where you could get good rye bread and dried apricots wrapped in butcher block paper and I would ride the elevator to the ninth floor in Bernadette's building which is where Bernadette's apartment was to hang out with her and Phil and sometimes the kids but usually the kids were busy doing kid things like exploring the subway tunnels to see who was living down there I swear to God and one time Max came home with an orange and green water pistol that was really more the size of a machine gun and he was spraying us all with water and this was often how it was at Bernadette's around the big wooden table in the dining room which was covered with stacks of papers of poems and kids' homework and Bernadette's freelance proofreading work and what I am saying is that it was never boring which made other people want to come there too, sometimes Dave and sometimes Laynie Browne who lived on East 7th Street with her cat Smokey and sometimes Kevin Davies who lived on Allen Street in an apartment building that had all Chinese residents except him who was Canadian because a previous resident had killed himself in Kevin's apartment and Kevin was pretty sure that now they only rented that particular apartment to Canadians and I should say right now that there were other important places to go in the neighborhood which were Kim's Video on Avenue A where a two-day movie rental was two dollars and it must have still been VHS tapes back then and there was also Habib's falafel stand where guys played impromptu jazz out on the sidewalk including Tony Garnier from Bob Dylan's band so I liked to stop by there *just in case* and also the pizza place on the southwest corner of Tompkins Square Park that was later replaced by something more fancy like maybe a French restaurant but while it was still a pizza place the pizza was $1.25 a slice and also of course there was St. Mark's Church where I'm pretty sure I saw John Ashbery read that summer and Gem Spa where I had my first egg cream which I was surprised to find out did not have eggs in it and just to review the math it was true that on any given day on the Lower East Side for three dollars and twenty-five cents there was a full evening of food and entertainment which was a slice of pizza and a movie from Kim's Video unless you wanted to add an egg cream or a beer or a martini at the Tile Bar which is what Kevin Davies and I especially liked to do that summer and one more thing about the cheap entertainment is that I should point out right now that I decided I wanted to watch all of Fellini's movies that summer and I'm not sure why except that they were dark and light and ecstatic and depressing at the same time, especially like the scene on the beach in *La Dolce Vita* where the sea monster is looking up with its dead eye at all the sexy Italians who really don't care about it very much but of course

49

it's also the case that there was something about the reckless love of Marcello Mastroianni that felt connected to the reckless love I had for and got from New York City and also that reminded me of the way poets could be reckless and compelling and kind of prickly like Stephen Rodefer for example who turned out to like European movies too especially the French ones where people had oral sex and in fact I would say that moving to New York kind of had that about it, a mix of the Good Life and the New Life like a cross between a Fellini movie and a Dante book, as in when Dante says of love, "Here is a god stronger than I, who shall come to rule over me" and that is what I was thinking about when I thought of New York when I first lived there that it was a god-stronger-than-I especially on the block between 7th and 8th and B and C where Laynie lived with Smokey the cat and across the street was the squatters' building where Brad Will had his pirate poet radio show and there were chickens and even a rooster on that block that you could hear all the way over to St. Brigid's Church where a couple years later we would all go to Elio Schneeman's funeral and there was a reception afterward in the basement that was very sad and that was one of many deaths around then around the time that the Lower East Side was about to be gentrified but it wasn't yet gentrified because just for a moment for example on Avenue C you could buy a live pigeon out of a box for dinner which reminds me about how later when I moved to Sunnyside in Queens Bernadette said that her high school boyfriend Bob Viscusi was from Sunnyside and his mother used to shoot pigeons from her fire escape window for dinner and I liked that story because it said something about the steady self-determination of poets and immigrants but I wondered where Bob Viscusi's mother got the shotgun and just with all of this you can see the sheer amount of mental processing it took to live in New

York not to mention the fact of the noise of the air conditioners in the air shafts and the fact that there was actually a movie being shot at night outside our window with a big spotlight on a crane and also once someone died in the building next door and we watched the little dented rusty coroner's van take the body away in a dark blue plastic body bag and all of that made me realize that as much as I loved New York I was also getting a little bit agoraphobic which is something I shared with Kevin Davies who lived on Allen Street and with Bernadette who lived on East 4th Street so Kevin suggested I take Valium and Bernadette suggested I see Dr. Fill who was her anthroposophical doctor whose office was on the Upper East Side and who was really old and German and when I asked him what was wrong with me he said that it was his opinion that when I woke up in the morning my soul didn't want to come back into my body from the astral plane because I frankly had too much going on and so he gave me an acupuncture treatment which I remember because he accidentally left some of the needles in my head like tiny horns and he also gave me an injection of something in a hypodermic needle and I asked him what is that and he said it's *Aurum* which I later found out was gold dust which didn't work as well as the Valium I got when I eventually went to the emergency room at St. Vincent's and said I thought I was having a heart attack but after I saw Dr. Fill I was really disturbed about my soul's intention not to live in my body so I went to the New York Public Library on 5th Avenue with the statues of the lions on the steps and I sat in the big wooden echoing reading room reading rare books by Rudolf Steiner which told me some things about orders of angels on the astral plane but I don't remember getting a lot of insights about what was really wrong with me and all of this reminds me of how much can happen in one day in New York City which is why the phrase "ecstatic connectedness" and also the word "entanglement" are in my mind right at this very moment because I think it's accurate to say that New York for me is all about an ecstatic connected entanglement that began for me through my friendship with Bernadette Mayer on the Lower East Side in the hot and humid summer of 1994 when O. J. Simpson was on the run in his white Ford Bronco and people like me who were agoraphobic hypochondriacs were worried about catching the flesh-eating virus and it's funny to think how such a confluence of things in a dirty city like New York could be the inspiration for things that look like pastoral odes from the English countryside but this is what happened for me when I started writing poems in New York and they became praise poems like Dante says for the city that came to rule over me because it was so strange and reckless like if a city was Marcello Mastroianni or Stephen Rodefer so when I wrote "O Life Force of Supernalness of World" and "Ye White Antarctic Birds" and "Poem Beginning with a Line by Frank Lima" and "O Razorback Clams" those were all written around 1995 or 1996 when New York and I were still in our honeymoon mode and this is what it sounds like to be on a honeymoon with a strange and reckless city, this is the poem called "Ye White Antarctic Birds" which is a poem that I wrote after going to see a show of Joe Brainard's collages with Anselm Berrigan at Tibor de Nagy Gallery in Midtown which was not long after Joe died which I also remember because there was a gigantic thunderstorm that swept over the city that afternoon and I always think of Joe as ascending to heaven up the rainbow that I saw on East 10th Street after that.

> Ye white antarctic birds of upper 57th street,
> you gallery of white antarctic birds, you
> street with white antarctic birds and

cabs and white antarctic birds you street,
ye and you the street and birds I walk upon
the galleries of streets and birds and longings,
you the birds antarctic of the conversations
and the bank machines, you the atm of
longing, the longing for the atm machines,
you the lover of banks and me and birds
and others too and cabs, and you the cabs
and you the subtle longing birds and me,
and you the conversations yet antarctic, and
soup and teeming white antarctic birds and
you the books and phones and atms the bank
machines antarctic, and you the banks and
cabs, and him the one I love, and those who
love me not, and all antarctic longings, and
all the birds and cabs and also on the street
antarctic of this longing.

And probably what I've been holding on to in my mind since I started writing this letter is that it is appropriate for me to be called a New York School poet which is not to disavow other things like the Black Mountain School or the Beats but to say that the poems I write which are recognizable as poems by Lisa Jarnot are New York School poems in the way that they move as for example here is the first New York School poem I ever wrote which is called "Dictionary" because of the game where you find an obscure word in the dictionary and everyone writes a fake definition for it and then you try to figure out which definition is the real one and which are the fake ones and you get points for faking people out and this is definitely a poem I wrote for Bernadette but I never wrote "for Bernadette" on it I just knew it was for her like when I later wrote

"Age of the Velocipede" I never wrote "for Anne Waldman" on it but I knew it was for Anne because it began with a line she wrote to me in the first postcard she ever sent to me which I kept on my desk which opened with the line "you are not a wounded animal" but to go back to the poem called "Dictionary" it sounds like this:

> As a small south american squirrel
> inhabiting mostly mountainous regions
> would feed on lizards half-way between
> poles of the tropics, I too would fall
> heartbreaked in the settlement of feuds
> or the fields of kentucky.
>
> When the moss grows high between the
> perennials and disordered mimmocks weep,
> these dainty fastidious gestating mammals
> break for leavened bread and sup between
> the rows of trees, lifting like friars
> some heavy books in sunlight's morning
> windows where the mollusks row in scion's
> quadragesimal phyla.

Which for me is a New York School poem for a couple reasons including the reason that I wrote it in New York and that it is a sonnet and I am pretty sure I wrote this sonnet at Bernadette's living room table on East 4th Street or if I didn't I definitely played the game of Dictionary there with her and probably Lee Ann Brown who first published Bernadette's *Sonnets* and definitely Bernadette's boyfriend Phil and maybe one or two of the kids played too because they were generally up for those kinds of things, playing Dictionary or watching basketball on TV which was hard to concentrate on because Bernadette was always yelling at the basket-ball players "Show us your cocks!" and I want to say that I finessed my love of sonnets there at Bernadette's apartment on East 4th Street where she wrote her book of sonnets that were wild free-range sonnets like Ted Berrigan's but Bernadette's were a little less angular than Ted's as if Ted had written his using a mechanical pencil and Bernadette had written hers using a crayon and they were dirty sonnets and daring sonnets and melancholy sonnets and there are a lot of Bernadette's sonnets that I particularly like and that are familiar like old sweaters and here is one of them and it's called "Sonnet":

> At 172 E. 4th Street near the bottom of NY's Avenue A
> Lights make black shadows of green trees
> And at noon they shout like cannibals
> They shout like birds for an hour at noon
> To watch the wind I will not go (outside my house)
> I can't, all night the night is going on
> The grand trees, school's closed, the phone bills
> Rhyme in three's and each of us takes turns being
> Jealous but it's I who have no stylus
> I can't hear symphonies, can't hear the popular
> Songs goodbye night you young men of morning
> Why don't you spend the hurricane with me
> Coming light your brand new flashlights a little bit
> Come on, be even more generous, you boys

The book of mine with the poem called "Dictionary" for Bernadette and "The Age of the Velocipede" for Anne was called *Ring of Fire*, which was named that at a bar on Avenue A across from Tompkins Square Park where Lee Ann and I once saw The Raincoats sing "Lola" but on this occasion I was there with Anselm Berrigan having a beer and I was asking what am I going to call this book and Johnny Cash's "Ring of Fire" came on the jukebox and there was no longer any doubt about the title and all those poems in that book were started when I started having an affair with New York City but a few were written when I was still married to Providence, Rhode Island where I had previously lived which was around the time that Brad Gooch's biography of Frank O'Hara came out and was being read by poets and I remember reading it and having it read to me in a bed full of naked people when I was still married to Providence and I thought that as much fun as Providence was New York City could be even more fun at least based on what I knew about it from Frank O'Hara's poems and in Providence we poets started using lines from Frank O'Hara's poems as code words like for example if you were in a public place with other people where you were supposed to be acting respectable you could still look at someone and say "ah, lunch" which was a way of telling them that you really wanted to sleep with them but what I really liked about Frank O'Hara was not just that he was dirty like New York but that he was transcendent like Joe Brainard floating to heaven on a rainbow and that was how Frank O'Hara's poems read to me so much so that I always wanted to find that gentle touch when I wrote but it was always just out of reach like in his poem "Avenue A"—

AVENUE A

We hardly ever see the moon any more
                               so no wonder
          it's so beautiful when we look up suddenly
     and there it is gliding broken-faced over the bridges

brilliantly coursing, soft, and a cool wind fans
　　　　your hair over your forehead and your memories
　　　　　　of Red Grooms' locomotive landscape
I want some bourbon/you want some oranges/I love the leather
　　　　　　jacket Norman gave me
　　　　　　　　　　　　　and the corduroy coat David
　　　gave you, it is more mysterious than spring, the El Greco
heavens breaking open and then reassembling like lions
　　　　　　　　　in a vast tragic veldt
　　　that is far from our small selves and our temporally united
passions in the cathedral of Januaries

　　　everything is too comprehensible
these are my delicate and caressing poems
I suppose there will be more of those others to come, as in the past
　　　　　　　　so many!
but for now the moon is revealing itself like a pearl
　　　　　　　　to my equally naked heart

—where I could see that life in New York wasn't just about lust and long-
ing it was also about revealing where God was sitting in the city, in the
cathedral of Januaries, and later I found this in James Schuyler's work
too, that there was a portal to the sublime in every mention of a street
tree so having explained this I can say now that I want to talk about the
feeling of falling in love that makes poetry possible but I also have to say
that it's not just one kind of love but many kinds of love, including the
gritty lusty love which might be Eros and the appreciation love which
C. S. Lewis talks about which is what I have for egg creams, an appre-
ciation love, and the sublime love that is more mysterious where you

sometimes get a glimpse of the Holy Spirit in a cityscape but it isn't going to entertain your desire for it to stick around long enough for you to transcribe it into your poem except if you are very lucky like Frank O'Hara was and also I think that what I learned from Bernadette was that you could maximize the chance of getting glimpses of that mystery by being a poet all the time and not just after going to school or clocking out of the office, that life was the poem and that the poem was life and that if someone told you it was stupid or useless you could just write a poem about that too, and my poems became more like that as well, like something that a kid said, like this poem of Bernadette's "Marie Makes Fun of Me at the Shore":

> Marie says
> look tiny red spiders
> are walking
> across the pools
> & just as I am writing down
> tiny red
> spiders are
> walking across the pools
> She says Mom I can just see it
> in your poem it'll say
> tiny red spiders are walking
> across the pools

And I know I said in a previous talk that the Steinian repetition in my work is not directly from Gertrude Stein but is from Robert Duncan writing derivations of Gertrude Stein and it's also the case that the Steinian repetition in my work is not from Gertrude Stein but is from Bernadette writing derivations of Gertrude Stein that weren't derivations of

Gertrude Stein at all because she started writing that way before she read Gertrude Stein and for example, this is how those derivations of derivations come into my work:

FOUND TEXT

The deer mistook their reflections for deer and the deer mistook their reflections for other deer and the deer apparently mistook their reflections for sheep and what the deer mistook their reflections for isn't certain and the deer were removed from the scene, being deer, before being removed and mistaking reflections of the other deer for the sheep the deer were removed and the deer deciding to join them joined the deer having mistaken reflections of sheep for the deer in the plate glass windows.

What I like about this poem is that both Bernadette and Lewis are haunting this poem and I haven't talked about Lewis yet, but I will and I will tell you that it is in this poem that I see Bernadette's form which is what I would call the slingshot method of the poem where the line gets wound tighter and tighter as it goes on and sometimes it is all released at the end like with a couplet that changes the energy and sometimes it is not released and it just stays tightly wound. But what I see in this poem is also Lewis's influence and now I am talking about Lewis Warsh and the way he helped me to understand many tricks about the content of a poem where in this case a newspaper article about the absurdity of modern life is the foundation of the narrative but it gets shredded up Dadaist-style into a collage but then it comes back together and gets held in place with Bernadette's trick of staying tightly wound with repetition and I'm talking about Lewis because I met him at the end of my first year in New York, through Bernadette, since they had once been married and had the children Marie and Sophia and Max and then I also met Anne through Lewis, because they had been married too but they didn't have children because Anne's mother told her she would kill her if she saw her pushing a baby carriage through the West Village and this is something that my friend the poet Jennifer Moxley from Providence warned me about right before I moved to New York where she didn't think I should go because it would wreck my poetry and my personal life and she said be careful about New York because terrible things happen there like people who have never met Allen Ginsberg refer to him as "Allen" and they write poems about their futons and they get involved in very complicated love affairs. She was very against the whole thing, of me going to New York and she was right about some things and when I called her on the phone sometimes from the Lower East Side she would say, "I told you so," and it's true I haven't forgotten any of those things which are also reflected in a poem I wrote in the style of Lewis that was based on actual events and I titled it "Autobiography":

> I didn't sleep with anyone for six months until I met X. While I was sleeping with Y I also slept with Y's girlfriend. While I was sleeping with Y's girlfriend I also slept with S and T. During the six months between sleeping with Y and sleeping with X I spent a lot of time with K. I never slept with K but J slept with K and Y's girlfriend and also with S. After leaving Y and before meeting X I didn't sleep with anyone for six months.

The variable named "X" in the poem was Lewis and I fell in love with him because he was somewhat tall and dark and handsome and also because there was something about him that was all poet, all writer, and also he was weirdly singularly dedicated to the confluence between Eros and Poetry in the way that maybe only a Scorpio can be though I didn't know all that at the time, I just got the vibe that there was something going on that was what my friend Jennifer had warned me against, which inspired me to write this poem for him called "Ode" sometime around the beginning of our relationship but I didn't say it was for Lewis because only I knew it was for Lewis:

ODE

For let me consider him who pretends to be the pizza delivery man and is instead the perfect part of day, for the fact he is a medium, for the eight to twelve inches of snow he tends to be, for he who covers the waterfront, for he that was handmade in a tiny village in japan, for that he is more than just an envelope or inside-out balloon, for that he can always find the scotch tape, for that he resembles a river in mid-december muddied over, for that he has seen the taxi cabs on fire in the rain, for that he is like the heat beneath the desk lamp, for that he is not a tiny teal iguana, for that it is he who waits for me inside cafes, for that he has hands and legs, for that he exceeds the vegetable, for that he is the rest of the balance continuing huge.

And when I remember being with Lewis I always remember that line in the lecture by Robert Duncan where he says "One-half of the world is looking for something nasty and one-half of the world is looking for something gnostic" which is also not just how my relationship with Lewis was, but how my relationship with New York was, that I was definitely learning to celebrate the low and the high, the nasty and the gnostic, the cannibals and the cathedrals in the poems that I wrote then a lot of times in conversation with Lewis's poems which were built off of a reporting style, and a direct address, and some mock-autobiographic turns that he used in his poems that let you know it was a poem by Lewis like in this poem he wrote called

The milk was sour, but I drank it anyway
You must check the expiration date on the container
    before you buy it
I spilled the container of sour milk into the sink
The strawberries are moldy, I only bought them
    yesterday
It's pointless to ruin your life over love for another
    person
You can always go back to the store and get a refund
I ran out into the rain and went to the store
    for a container of milk
It's not necessary to wear clothing when you go
    to the store
No one in the store notices whether you're wearing
    clothing or not
For some animals the ritual pattern of courtship
    is a dance of death
Wet streets, the entrance to the bridge, the windows
    of stores selling diamonds
Go back to where you started and repeat everything
    you said
Once I stood where Mao stood and stared down at
    Tiananmen Square
And once the wind blew me backwards off the Great Wall

And around the time that Lewis and I started dating was around the time
he had just gotten back from the Great Wall and also Tibet where he
rode in an airplane where they served a lunch that was hot dogs in a

Dixie cup and his books *Avenue of Escape* and *Private Agenda* were published around then too which are both titles that say something about his insistent mysterious Scorpio nature but also I was always surprised by how funny his poems were too like in the first poem in *Avenue of Escape* where he slips in the line "The woman upstairs says she thinks her dog found something that resembles a gerbil & ate it" and when I read that I just couldn't help but love him especially in the way the gerbil line was followed by a reflection on Nietzsche and this ongoing conversation between my poetry and Lewis's poetry continued in the flash fictions that we wrote together, except for now I can only find my half of those collaborations which sound like this:

> One Saturday in July the cable man came to the door and she let him in. Once he was standing on the edge of the balcony and he saw a dog-headed man on the beach. Every Wednesday the phone rang and someone named Vegas left a message for someone named Cynthia about the cast parties at the Python Club. It was that simple but somehow it seemed all wrong.

Those days when I looked for myself in Lewis's work I mostly just saw his other girlfriends reflected back at me but these days I see the way he loved both the nasty and gnostic mysteries of relationships and was always looking for the one that would break the mold but to change the subject again the story in the poem about the man seeing the dog-headed man on the beach was a true story about Lewis thinking he saw a dog-headed man on the beach since his eyes were never very good and that was when we were on vacation at the Captain's Bounty motel in Rockport, Massachusetts, when he stood on the balcony at dusk one night and said, "I just saw a dog-headed man on the beach," and it made me think of a collage by Helen Adam and the motel had a statue of a pirate in front of it and balconies on the back overlooking the Atlantic and it was kind of trashy and kind of spooky at the same time and what I remember about that trip is that we went on a whale watch and saw either right or minke whales or maybe both and also in Rockport I got sick from eating shellfish and spent a whole night throwing up and Lewis berated me for being sick, insisting it was another sign of my depressive nature, that I just couldn't have a good time even on vacation and we also went to Dogtown in Gloucester and Lewis took a photograph of me standing over a gravestone that said MOTHER in all caps.

It was Lewis who told me I was a lazy writer which I wasn't sure if I agreed with, but later I found out he told Anne that he thought I was a talented writer but I never knew that until she mentioned it very recently and it made me really miss him and the way we lived together among the history of his friendships with Ted and Alice and Allen and Ron and Larry and Tom and Bill and Joe and Kenward and George and Katie, and there was a way in which each and every line of the poems of the New York School were transmitted into our conversations which is why I was there in the first place because I am more prone to the anecdotal than the academic, so what was of ultimate value to me was information about the way Tom Clark posed for a picture, or which books Ted stole from Lewis and Bernadette's bookshelves, or what happened at 33 St. Mark's Place when Anne and Lewis lived there together and what movies were going to influence Lewis's next book *A Place in the Sun* which meant we had to spend weeks watching movies with Montgomery Clift and Elizabeth Taylor including *Suddenly, Last Summer* which we watched while sitting on Max's bed eating watermelon, so to go back to it when he said I was lazy I was actually probably the opposite, I was very busy gathering information and working very hard watching movies with

Montgomery Clift and eating watermelon with Lewis and eventually writing a poem called "Suddenly, Last Summer" which is another poem about the summer in New York City like the first summer I lived there on East 6th Street between Avenues A and B but is also about the movie with Montgomery Clift where in the final scene on the beach the poet is torn to shreds and eaten by the cannibalistic lovers like the burning heart of Dante that Beatrice also eats:

> Sun worshipper I, in the absence of the sun, in the
> things I don't remember, the unfriendliness of night,
> the neon night and blue blue night, the creatures
> on the beach,
>
> Suddenly, to remember the sun and all the creatures
> on the beach, suddenly to remember the sun and
> little sunstroked turtles, suddenly the neon night
> surrounding little turtles all surrounded by the night
> upon the turtles on the beach,
>
> Sea creatures and mergansers, the blue blue night,
> the turtles on the beach all worshipping Apollo, suddenly
> I am thrown into your library, never to be what I was
> before, surrounded by a tiny light inside the dark and
> clutching little turtles,
>
> Go back upon the beach and remember the sun,
> suddenly, surrounded by neon, go back, go back to the
> beach and worship it, go back to what I was before,
> a worshipper upon the beach, Apollo's, in the lavender,
> beside mergansers at the sea's night shore.

IV

IS THAT A REAL POEM OR
DID YOU JUST MAKE IT UP?

I wrote this on a train from New York City to Chicago and I was feeling at least a little bit melancholy maybe because of the autumn season that seriously lacks autumnal weather or maybe because of traveling away from things familiar in a time of such great social instability or maybe because of the closure of this series of talks that have occupied my imagination for the last couple of years. This is the final lecture in this series that began in October of 2020 at the Poetry Project in New York City. That talk was about my origins as a person in a little town in upstate New York called Derby, and about my origins as a poet in the neighboring city of Buffalo where I went to college.

So this talk calls back to those origins and it delves into endings as well. This is also a place to explore my first book, *Some Other Kind of Mission*, which was written in the early 1990s and published in 1996 by Keith and Rosmarie Waldrop at Burning Deck Press, and my most recent book, *A Princess Magic Presto Spell*, written over a period of a decade between 2009 and 2019 and published by my friend Devin Johnston of Flood Editions. I would happily say this latter book ends my life's work as a poet not to be overly dramatic or grim but to acknowledge the satisfaction I have with the work as an ending point: where I can say, yes, this is a real book and I did make it up.

When I was on the train leaving New York City writing this lecture I was looking at the cattails in the marshlands of the Hudson Valley near Bear Mountain, and I was thinking about the idea of first things and final things, not particularly in relation to my own life, but in relation to the Holocene extinction event that is upon us, which feels to me like the universe's attempt to make up a new and different poem out of a troubled world.

I have my own upstate New York origin story that contributes to the first things of my poems: gravel driveways, snowy owls, willow trees, mourning doves, football, a bowling alley, Jell-O, and Campbell's soup. It's pretty down-home stuff, pretty Americana. My old friend and mentor, the poet Jack Clarke, called it the Derby Shuffle, the way I and my poems make our way along through this lifespan. I knew what he meant then, as I said in the first talk in this series. It meant that I wasn't going to be a fancy academic poet, nor should I want to—and I understand the nuance of what he meant even more now: that over time what I've done as a poet comes out of the guts of the origin story, that at the matrix of the messy mix of snowy owls and Campbell's soup, I've developed an ear for the mystery that brings all those elements together into the creation. It's not a rarefied gift. Here I'd return to a line of Spinoza's: that prophecy (or poetry) "implies not a peculiarly perfect mind, but a peculiarly vivid imagination," which usually is not worth much of anything in our culture.

I'm thinking of a phrase from the Book of Revelation: what does it mean for the poet to act as prophet in imagining a new heaven and a new earth? Both *Some Other Kind of Mission* and *A Princess Magic Presto Spell* hold keys to that question for me because they are books that began with the intention of imagining a new heaven and a new earth. The goal of those projects was not just to record events in the world or to create an imitation of life, as Aristotle says in his *Poetics*, but to see the undersides and oversides of this multiverse that we inhabit. That might sound like something a fancy poet would say, but what I really mean is something simple: the going reality for me of the rocks and gravel and snowy owls and Jell-O and Campbell's soup that occupies my origin story brought with it a feeling that there were mysteries outside of the seen world. The poem is not only something I make up, it is also something that makes itself revealed: it is a manifestation of life, a revelation of another order, a new heaven and a new earth, a breakthrough event where the divine streams in. Again, let's stop here as what I just said raises the red flag of a fancy metaphysical Neoplatonic Duncanian spiritual idea of what poetry is, but I would like to explore it also from a more practical angle, not from Robert Duncan's metaphysics but from Wallace Stevens's more sober psychoanalytic reading (which is still a little metaphysical). Stevens writes in his essays on poetics of the power of the poem that it is "a violence from within that protects us from a violence without. It is the imagination pressing back against the pressure of reality."

That tension is very real for me: between the imagination and reality, or, as I would also put it, between the sacred and the secular, or between the eternal and the temporal orders. Because I always experienced the day-to-day status quo of American life as a violence, I was more than willing to jump into life as a poet and a life where the imagination could press back against that reality, as Stevens insisted. In the process I also found that it's not just the violence of the imagination that protects us from an external violence, it's also the tenderness of the imagination that bears witness to the pathos of the real, of the profane, of the temporal.

My first book, *Some Other Kind of Mission*, was built as a puzzle to tease out that tension between the sacred and the profane, and it was very much influenced by the poet Jack Spicer's idea of poetry as magic and the poet Robert Duncan's idea of poetry as revelation of a world. I was looking for an answer to a question or to several questions. On a personal, more mundane level I was looking for an answer to a question about a doomed love affair. But on another level I was looking for a confirmation that the combination of language and imagination could redeem me, could get me out of the pickle I was in in my relationship to the real: both in relation to my personal relationships and in relation to the violent landscape of my culture. I was looking to create a world that would buffer me, envelop me, reveal to me a higher order. I was then a fairly staunch atheist, but in retrospect I can see now that I was also seeking divine intervention or revelation of the divine which at the time given my poetical interests probably would've looked more like the intervention of a Greek God than a Christian God.

When I went back to this book, *Some Other Kind of Mission*, I found a beautiful passage nestled in the final long poem that reminds me of what I was looking for and how I actually found it. Maybe it is Eros or maybe it is the Christ that I'm speaking of. I do know that partly this passage is a record of a dream I had about thirty years ago:

> It was then that I realized I would be on a train. In the hallway. It was at the end of the road. And that's how I knew I would always find it. It had water instead of a road. It was a river. But not the ocean. It had balconies. But a real house. A house that people live in. He thought I was poor. And in his house. It had long lists written in red. He left me in his house. Or that was my construction. But He had left me in his house. It was a crowded street with many houses. With the river plus balconies. The house became water. The road would enter a bigger road. At the edge of the road later was another house.

I think of poetry as a process of building boats and building houses and making storehouses and treasuries. Staying busy building an eternal boat is exactly what I'm doing in the poem. The practical aspects of *Some Other Kind of Mission*, the compositional decisions, emerged out of uneasiness I had about poems in that moment. I had taken a liking to Jack Spicer's proposition that the poem was a conjuring device: it frustratingly approached the real—but the divine in language, the Logos, was nearly impossible to pin down in our sad, human, low ghost language and imaginations. I had started to make Super 8 films to see if I could capture that Logos in moving images. I had begun to record soundscapes around me. I was on a road trip with friends to North Carolina one Christmas when the narrative of the main prose components of the book came into shape while I was looking out the window of a little Honda Accord at the red clay embankments of the South:

> Blood in my eyes followed by truck in motel. either severely or proper. followed by police activity. followed by truck in. followed by followed by. followed by truck in motel. at the library. at the truck in motel. at the of. today there where they're taking me. followed by. i dreamt about and followed by a truck in thence motel. followed by properly. car construction cup against. in the heron squared. in some other cities. in the dream in the car in the truck of. up against the car. against construction against the truck. followed by the meticules of fall out. up again the car the truck. when i turned my head. as for my partner. followed by truck in motel. and i knew it was turning my head in construction of carp. up against the carp construction. up against the car constructed meticules of famous carp.

It was a conjuring. It was the beginning of a creation of a world that included some of the elements of my origin story, the rocks and the gravel, now accompanied by the trucks and motels and herons and carp. The prose sections of the book were collaged against visual poems that were in some ways transcripts of Super 8 films and sound recordings. The book opens with an homage to Homer, to Eros, and to the violence of the real, with a collage listing the names of World War II airplanes: Messerschmitts, B-17s, Spitfires, and Zeros, and the lines "Give Helen back, or some other kind of mission." Throughout the long, intermingled road-trip prose section there's a turning back to the language of creation, of the mix of rocks and gravel that make a solid road, all haunted by the decay of America and the silent watching trees.

I think the power of the poem for me is its ability to exercise authority over what I call in one prose section of this book "the target in the marketplace next to near the temple of the void." When I brought parts of this book-in-progress to a classroom of fellow students in about 1993 at Brown University, one of them said in exasperation, "It reads like the plans of the quiet guy next door who builds bombs," and I thought, That's exactly what I want it to do. I want it to blow up the cultural complacency. I want it to target the marketplace, the satanic commodity culture, and to expose the temple of the void that we worship in the form of global capitalism. I don't think I would have been able to articulate all this when I was twenty-four and writing this book, but I had a passion and I had an intuition, and I was led along by the prophetic around me in a tradition that included the work Allen Ginsberg did in "Howl" to blow up Moloch, to take on the giant.

The title of this talk comes from a story I remember the poet Bob Creeley telling, about an audience member at a reading asking him, "Is that a real poem or did you just make it up?" After all these years my memory fails me and I'm not sure if it was him who was asked this question or if he was relating the story of another poet being asked this question. All I know is it happened to a poet at a poetry reading and I love the question because the obvious answer is "Yes, I just made it up because I had a feeling about the potentiality of a new heaven and a new earth and I want to inhabit it."

I had a feeling there was something beyond the actual Walmart on the highway. The easy way to describe it is to call it the Eternal, the thing that we know is there outside of us, though Jack Spicer says that there are many ways we can describe that "something beyond." He suggests we could call it the Martians or the Id, but he was a good Calvinist, so I suspect he knew it could also be a thing called God. And I don't mind calling it God or Creation, a mystery that we get a glimpse of here and there that shines through events and language.

My latest book, *A Princess Magic Presto Spell*, in its very title gives an indication that this Spicerian drama has never left my craftwork, my boat-building endeavors. What I wanted to write was James Schuyler's *A Few Days* or Bernadette Mayer's *Midwinter Day* and of course Anne Waldman's *Iovis* comes to mind as does the *Cantos* and the question of what the *Cantos* would look like if it were written by a woman and particularly by a mom, so at the beginning of this project, the *Cantos* was always in the back of my mind and unconsciously elements of the Homeric epic came into the book also, just as they had with *Some Other Kind of Mission*. But beyond these vague desires, there was no road map for *A Princess Magic Presto Spell*. I decided that when I could, on any given day, I would write down a phrase of exactly three words, and I began that practice while largely socially isolated caring for a few-week-old baby, my daughter Beatrice, who was a world unto herself, who had arrived as a beacon from another world, and it may be that I thought it

would be useful to record for her something of that time that we had to-
gether right at the beginning of her origin story. I wanted to create a me-
morial to life emerging:

Into the eve of a picnic of trees of the Strawberry Rugulet Rabbit Tyrone

was the beginning of this new world written in Homeric dactyls, full of
resonances of the landscape of a one-bedroom rental apartment in
Queens over a loud Dominican bodega. Structurally the project became
a collage of an entirely different kind than *Some Other Kind of Mission*.
In that first book the collage elements had hard visible edges; there were
bumps in the road. In *A Princess Magic Presto Spell* those edges were
blended together like a river flowing, winding across time and space. I
gave it no direction. There was only revelation. It was like my child, who
was at the center of the work. No matter what plan I had there was no
plan: there was only a revelation of her life force and I followed it. Poems
always function the same way for me. They are autonomous and other-
worldly. In its autonomy, *A Princess Magic Presto Spell* became something
both expected and unexpected.

Into the eve of a picnic of trees of the Strawberry Rugulet Rabbit Tyrone
into a glazed economic disturbance caused by the rain most dramatic and
strange

The poem begins with that dactylic couplet, and then it breaks into bite-
sized amounts of sleep-deprived dailiness:

small whole moon in the sky   fishlike in semblance
as damp as an amphibrach the Anthony Braxton gland of ant launch

wind blown shutters   angry household gods
wet September horses

What I didn't anticipate were the other elements of Homeric epic that would emerge along the way: tributes to those born into the culture of the poem, into my child's generation: Yuki Lily Atkins, Vivian Rose Champion, Adrian Walker Bruza Koch, a baby named Ellington, a midsummer kitten; elegies to those poet-prophets who died during that decade: Michael Gizzi, Tuli Kupferberg, Bruce Kurland, Ray DiPalma, Anselm Hollo, Stephen Rodefer, Bill Kushner, Larry Fagin, Peter Culley, Jack Collom, Bobbie Louise Hawkins, Bill Corbett, and Tom Gizzi. The naming of "Gods" arrived, figures not always of particular significance to me, but for some reason making their appearance known with proper three-word epithets like Gray-Eyed Athena: Shy Franz Schubert, Lonely Frank O'Hara, Poor Franz Kafka, Sweet Paul Celan. The pathos of the gods, the absurdity of the news headlines, my child's first words, and phrases misheard all emerging together out of the push and pull between the world of the living and the world of the dead.

It would be a mistake to let the Americana that I'm talking about sit on its romantic pedestal. At no point in bringing a child into the world could I turn away from the fearful lack of repentance that has doomed our culture. From my Derby Shuffle adjacent to the Seneca Nation to Charles Olson's westward sprawl to Robert Duncan's mysterious Golden Gate to Frank O'Hara's dirty New York City, there is always something amiss. Those cattails waving in the marshy field, the snowy owl and the willow tree and the myriad stars in the sky and the Jell-O and the Campbell's soup and the genocidal tendencies of a global super-predator known as *Homo sapiens*. That push and pull, that tension, and that conversation between the eternal and the temporal, between the sacred and the profane is the spark for my poems, and those tensions pressed me into the form of a poet. Cattails interrupted by a red stop sign interrupted by a car, or many cars like bees on the highway. The melancholy returns:

Teeming with life

        a midsummer kitten
            Mars hangs low
                over guns, rape, and great white sharks

Teeming with life,

        the sumac trees
        lighting Flushing Bay,

                rendered into death   the angel Moroni

Teeming with life:

        roaches, fruit flies, ants,
        hairballs, ringworm, fleas,

                Dr. Pee Sample's   elevated bilirubin,

                    From Graubins to Lederer
                    From Lercher to Mlinko

Teeming with life an Oval Pigtoe an Arkansas Fatmucket a Cumberland
   Monkeyface

                Over the road,   Harvey, Jack, and Bob,
                              Robert, Jess, and Stan,

                                            the Dog Days
                                        and then Rodefer

                                                        If you speak Chinese
                                                                press 22

                                        become a dementia swimming officer
                                                        a blue Reed's
                                                        Lou mask

        Teeming with life—
                Simita Ben Mocha

                                        a thing in
                                        a castle in
                                        a Kafka story

        Being in life
                sound bytes, iPhones, psyches

        fussy German beekeeper may you live in interesting times

                with global liquidity funds, south African asparagus,
                with rigid bureaucratic behavior
                for God, Han, Hannah
                and also for Bill Kushner

                for "emancipated" read "emaciated" in the
                        Georgia pine woods or

                                a little boat
                                in rainy weather

under the drawbridge
on Grand Avenue
the Metro Dong Ferry

for "Hopkinsesque" read "urinalysis"
and a pear-shaped white lady
crafted from the pelts
of North American coyotes

office max
copy max
furniture max

the last days of
the Standard Enzyme Company
uniquely positioned to
not miss Larry

Teeming with life
these sober engines dreaming

the last days of
the rare full moon
of Christmas Eve
in Galesburg,

for "garage" read "carnage"

The real melancholy is knowing that this experiment is coming to an end. Not just the poem, the life's work, or the individual lives, but the grain elevators, the bridges, a Manifest Destiny cursed from the beginning with a greed that was called progress at the expense of all else. An extinction event, the sixth and largest. The prophetic in my poetry is the acknowledgment of that. The melancholy is the mixed sadness and joy that what we share in this moment is bearing witness to an unfolding drama, a new cosmic poem. That which has been absurd and unsustainable is also to be washed away.

How does it feel to be a global super-predator barreling across the country on Joe Biden's Amtrak? In my church community the members of African descent refer to people of European descent in this country as the 1619 virus. The reparations they wait for likely will only come in the form of rising sea levels which eliminate all of us super-predators.

Outside Waterloo, Indiana, I hear the question James Joyce asked, "When will the Finnegans Wake?" The cannon in the town square idyllic like a jigsaw-puzzle vista, sinister too, the cities on the hills on this continent. The melancholy is real. The beauty of this place and its fragility. That is how the process of making the poem is for me: today I would turn Ted Berrigan's feminine, marvelous, and tough to my own melancholic, beautiful, and fragile, to look at the beauty of decay and change and to intuit the Sublime Porte of the poem where dust becomes spirit and spirit becomes dust, where dust and spirit meet. The final section of *A Princess Magic Presto Spell* reveals that story:

> Dust and spirit
> in the cavernous eyes
> of our dead cat
> help to immanentize the eschaton
> toward a fruit-based strangeness
> with the head of a girl
> with the snake of a body
> at the Erie County Fair

in the Synod of Dort
        find a solitude,
near the chessmen and the tax returns
        where the lammas dream

    in a luxury gay space communism
    find a dead wood's postcolonial guerilla exegesis

  in the mobs of vindicators
find the root fallacy
      of the music that can carry it

    and for "weird but true"
    read "the world tree"

                read the crows of Boulder,
              read the magpies of London,
        read archaic tribal garbage   or an original
            Christology
         and then Jack, and then Bobbie,
          and then Jeffrey's bridge,
         and then Corbett's ashes,

   in the funerals, dentists, divorces,
  in the brain masala and bhima astrologers
    be a brilliant heliotrope in a flannel waffle hemp

read the welfare queen's strawberry unicorn cakes   her bare buick rusting

     no Ding Dongs,
     no Sea Gods,
  and more Toms outbound.

SELECTED BIBLIOGRAPHY

AND WORKS CITED

Bruce, Lenny. *The Best of Lenny Bruce*. Fantasy Records, 1962.

Brueggemann, Walter. *The Practice of Prophetic Imagination*. Minneapolis: Fortress Press, 2012.

Clarke, John. *Tramping the Bulrushes*. New York: Spuyten Duyvil, 2017.

Creeley, Robert. *The Collected Poems of Robert Creeley, 1945–1975*. Berkeley: University of California Press, 1982.

Duncan, Robert. *Derivations: Selected Poems, 1950–1956*. London: Fulcrum Press, 1968.

———. *Fictive Certainties: Essays*. New York: New Directions, 1985.

———. *The First Decade: Selected Poems, 1940–1950*. London: Fulcrum Press, 1968.

———. *The H.D. Book*. Eds. Michael Boughn and Victor Coleman. Berkeley: University of California Press, 2011.

———. *The Opening of the Field*. New York: Grove Press, 1960.

Dylan, Bob. *The Times They Are A-Changin'*. Columbia, 1964.

Ginsberg, Allen. *Collected Poems, 1947–1980*. New York: Viking, 1985.

———. *Journals: Early Fifties, Early Sixties*. Ed. Gordon Ball. New York: Grove Press, 1978.

Jarnot, Lisa. *Black Dog Songs*. Chicago: Flood Editions, 2003.

———. *Night Scenes*. Chicago: Flood Editions, 2008.

———. *A Princess Magic Presto Spell: Parts 1–9*. Chicago: Flood Editions, 2019.

————. *Ring of Fire*. Boston: Zoland Books, 2001.

————. *Robert Duncan: The Ambassador from Venus: A Biography*. Berkeley: University of California Press, 2012.

————. *Sea Lyrics*. New York: Situations Press, 1996.

————. *Some Other Kind of Mission*. Providence: Burning Deck Press, 1996.

Kerouac, Jack. *The Dharma Bums*. New York: Viking, 1958.

Mayer, Bernadette. *A Bernadette Mayer Reader*. New York: New Directions, 1992.

Melville, Herman. *Moby-Dick*. New York: The New American Library, 1961.

O'Hara, Frank. *The Collected Poems of Frank O'Hara*. Ed. Donald Allen. Berkeley: University of California Press, 1995.

Rodefer, Stephen. *Four Lectures*. Berkeley: The Figures, 1982.

Spinoza, Benedict de. *A Theologico-Political Treatise and A Political Treatise*. Trans. R. H. M. Elwes. Mineola, NY: Dover, 2004.

Stevens, Wallace. *The Necessary Angel: Essays on Reality and the Imagination*. New York: Knopf, 1951.

Waldman, Anne. *The Iovis Trilogy: Colors in the Mechanism of Concealment*. Minneapolis: Coffee House Press, 2011.

Warsh, Lewis. *Alien Abduction*. New York: Ugly Duckling Presse, 2015.

Whitehead, Alfred North. *Process and Reality: An Essay in Cosmology*. New York: Macmillan, 1929.

Bruce Kurland's work can be viewed at: www.americanart.si.edu/artist/bruce-kurland-2744 and www.burchfieldpenney.org/art-and-artists/people/profile:bruce-kurland/#bruce-kurland

ACKNOWLEDGMENTS

The Bagley Wright Lecture Series on Poetry supports contemporary poets as they explore in depth their own thinking on poetry and poetics and give a series of lectures resulting from these investigations.

This work evolved from lectures given at the following institutions and organizations: "White Males, White Whales, Whitehead" at the Poetry Project, via Zoom, October 7, 2020; "White Males, White Whales, Whitehead" at Harvard Divinity School, via Zoom, December 2, 2020; "White Males, White Whales, Whitehead" at Woodland Pattern Book Center, via Zoom, December 17, 2020; "Abandon the Creeping Meatball: An Anarcho-Spiritual Treatise" at University at Buffalo, via Zoom, February 18, 2021; "Do You Agree or Disagree with Aristotle's Poetics?: On Forms and Emptiness" at the Iowa Writers' Workshop, via Zoom, April 30, 2021; "Do You Agree or Disagree with Aristotle's Poetics?: On Forms and Emptiness" at University of Washington Bothell, via Zoom, May 4, 2021; "Do You Agree or Disagree with Aristotle's Poetics?: On Forms and Emptiness" at Uppsala University, via Zoom, May 10, 2021; "On the Metaphysics of Deep Gossip" at Naropa University, via Zoom, June 24, 2021; "Is That a Real Poem or Did You Just Make It Up?" with Devin Johnston and Flood Editions at Subterranean Books, St. Louis, MO, September 30, 2021; "Is That a Real Poem or Did You Just Make It Up?" at Literary Arts, Portland, OR, via Zoom, December 9, 2021.

Thank you to Kyle Dacuyan at the Poetry Project; Ariella Ruth Goldberg, Charles Stang, and Corey O'Brien at Harvard Divinity School; Michael Wendt at Woodland Pattern Book Center; Liz Park, Emily Reynolds, and James Maynard at the University at Buffalo; Elizabeth Willis at the Iowa Writers' Workshop;

Jeanne Hueving and Amaranth Borsuk at University of Washington Bothell; Daniel Kane at Uppsala University; Jeffrey Pethybridge and Anne Waldman at Naropa University; Devin Johnston at Flood Editions and Kelly von Plonski at Subterranean Books; Jessica Meza-Torres and Susan Moore at Literary Arts; and all of their respective teams, for welcoming the Bagley Wright Lecture Series into their programming and for collaborating on these events. The Series would be impossible without such partnerships.

NOTE FROM THE AUTHOR

This book is the product of a community. Many thanks to Charlie Wright, Ellen Welcker, Heidi Broadhead, Joseph Gaglione, Sarah Sohn, Elizabeth Willis, Aaron Lercher, Devin Johnston, Daniel Kane, Lee Ann Brown, Laynie Browne, Jerry Reisig, Anne Waldman, Penelope Creeley, the late Charlie Palau, and all the audiences who attended these talks. Deep gratitude to and for my daughter Beatrice Evans who provides daily inspiration.